W9-BEY-767

THE GENUINE JESUS

Received by James E. Padgett
and Daniel G. Samuels

Compiled by Alan Ross

Edited by Lawrence Friedmam

Copyright © 1998 by Alan Ross

All rights reserved apart from any fair dealing for the
purposes of private study, research, criticism or review as
permitted under the Copyright Act, no part may be
reproduced or transmitted without prior written permission

ISBN: 0-9617038-2-2
Contains Bibliographical References

Ross Publications
734 1/2 New York Street
West Palm Beach, Florida 33401

www.thegenuinejesus.com
561 833-0384   alanross@aol.com

Printed in the USA and the UK

DEDICATION

I dedicate this book to my dearest friends of this spiritual path.
To Patricia Doyle, who was my first teacher, to Greg Boster,
who gave me my first book of writings, to Isaiah Watkins,
who was a spiritual father to me, and to Alese Jones,
whose help and encouragement has meant so much to me.

CONTENTS

Contents

THE REAPPEARANCE

THE SECOND COMING

THE TEACHINGS

PREFACE

The Genuine Jesus is a unique work in that it is the channeled story of Jesus' life presented in the first person, as it was received from him by two American mediums, James E. Padgett and Daniel G. Samuels.

The original writings used to create this story were given to the mediums over a period of many years and not in any particular order. Therefore, I have organized the material for this book in the order to follow the events of his life as recorded in the New Testament of the Bible. This book traces his life from his birth and youth to his ministry, death and resurrection. All of the material for this book originated from Jesus, except for some portions that came from other spirits who were present as mortals at the time the events of this story took place.

There are two hundred Bible references, that have been verified using the King James version. Some of these passages are not exact biblical quotes, but refer to Bible passages that the reader can use as a reference point when comparing this book to the New Testament.

In *The Genuine Jesus* there are concepts about his life and about his teachings that, to my knowledge, are not to be found elsewhere. The reader is asked to keep an open mind to things not found in the Bible or in other spiritual literature.

i

INTRODUCTION

Since his appearance in Palestine over two thousand years ago the story of the man from Galilee has spread to all corners of the world. His life has inspired artists and musicians to reach new heights. Great houses of worship have been erected to his glory, all in adoration of him for having lived a perfect life.

Who, then, was this man? Was he the result of a virgin birth? Is he God incarnate to be worshiped? Did he come to die on a cross for sin? Jesus states in this book that these things are all wrong. He was not born of a virgin, but in the normal way. He is not God and does not want to be worshiped. He did not come to die on the cross to pay a price for sin, but he died because of sin. His mission was to announce that God's love was now available and that he was the first to obtain through prayer an immortal soul filled with the Essence of God—Divine Love. It was in this way that he became the Christ, the promised Messiah and the first true son of God.

Jesus did sacrifice himself, but in a way that was never relayed or understood by the Gospel writers. He gave up the opportunity to have a home and family of his own and lead the quiet pursuits of a Nazarene carpenter. Instead, he endured the hatred and opposition of those who did not understand him and were threatened by him. He lived a life of constant travel, often without having a place to lay his head.

Jesus states that the doctrine of his blood sacrifice is just one of many that are pure speculation on the part of the Church fathers and cannot be satisfactorily explained. Their followers are told to accept this doctrine on faith alone, but, for many, faith was not enough as an explanation. These people, myself included, have sought answers outside the Bible and the established churches.

In 1982 my search for answers led me to a small group of Spiritualists where I was living in Santa Cruz, California. Their faith was based on a spiritual event that had taken place at the height of Spiritualism popularity, but had gone virtually unnoticed. It took the form of extraordinary, channeled writings originating from Jesus and his disciples.

In an early message, Jesus states, "The work I am now engaged in represents a new and important revelation from the world of spirit." Once again, Jesus had come to the earth, only this time in spirit form from his home high up in the heavens to be close to a certain Washington, DC, lawyer whom he used to record his thoughts by the means of automatic writing.

James Padgett had been a practical lawyer for thirty

five years prior to the development of his mediumship. Padgett was not a Spiritualist, but a Methodist. His mediumship began in 1914 shortly after his wife Helen's passing. Padgett loved Helen dearly, and her loss left a great void in his life. A friend who knew of his loneliness had been urging him to attend

James E. Padgett

a spiritualist meeting in the hope of making contact with her. Although reluctant, having been raised in the Protestant Church, he eventually agreed to accompany his friend to a meeting held at the home of a Mrs. Maltby.

There the medium described his wife perfectly to him and told him that she wanted to contact him from the spirit world and that she (the medium) recognized that he had the ability to write thoughts from his wife. In the evenings that followed, Padgett sat patiently at his desk with pencil in hand thinking of Helen and longing for contact. Many nights passed with no results, until one evening his hand moved and produced what he called "fish hooks and hangers". With practice he was able to write a short note signed Helen. In it she encouraged her husband to continue his efforts to receive her thoughts and to believe that it was really she.

Padgett was of course skeptical that the communications were truly from his deceased wife. So, he asked for proof. Helen responded by sending facts about their life together that Padgett recognized only the two of them had known. At first he thought the information was coming from his own mind or subconscious, but he soon dispelled that thought, for many of the things written he had forgotten long ago, and besides, only Helen would have re-called the details.

Padgett began reading books on Spiritualism and attending meetings where he was advised to continue taking messages while learning more about spirit communication and the spirit world. Prior to the writing sessions Padgett expressed that he could feel his wife's presence intensely, which brought him great happiness. In time he had no choice, but to accept the writings as proof that his wife was alive and well, fully conscious, living in another dimension, and that she was able to send her thoughts to him, and he was able to write them down.

Helen's letters then took a turn from the personal to the spiritual. She informed her husband that his ability to write messages from spirits was known in the highest realms of the spirit world and that Jesus and his disciples wanted to use his ability to bring spiritual knowledge to the world. Soon after, Padgett wrote a message from Jesus stating, that he had been trying for centuries to find an instrument that he could use to record his thoughts to correct what had been recorded in the New Testament about his life and his mission on earth.

Padgett had not been selected because he was more spiritually evolved compared to other men, for there were many others who were more advanced than he. But it was because he possessed a natural psychic gift that could be developed, and he had the ability to make his mind completely passive to allow the spirits' thoughts to pass through his brain uninterrupted, and to move his hand by spirit overshadowing to write their messages accurately.

Padgett was instructed through his writings to pray often for God's love to enter his soul and increase his psychic power. This would give his mediumship a higher quality of receptivity. His devotion to this work enabled him to create the optimum conditions by purifying his mind of material thoughts in order for him to receive every nature of intellectual, moral and spiritual knowledge.

After Jesus completed his great messages, his disciples and other spirits were allowed to take advantage of Padgett's ability. In one such message from John, the apostle, he describes Jesus' physical appearance.

John states, "I have never heard of any portrait having been painted of Jesus while he lived on earth. The oldest portraits in existence of him were not made until years after his death and by men who could not have gotten a description of him from anyone who had seen him.

"Nevertheless, as were the rest of us who were his disciples, the Master was a Jew, although, he was not typical, for he had a condition of soul that, to a large extent, determined and fashioned his appearance. His eyes were not dark or brown, but a violet blue. His hair was light and inclined to be auburn. He wore it parted in the middle, and it reached to his shoulders and was somewhat wavy, a beautiful head of hair that seemed to be full of life.

"His nose was straight and prominent, his beard was the color of his hair. His forehead was not very high or broad, but was well shaped and somewhat effeminate. Surprisingly, this was an indication that he did not have as much mental development as one might suppose, but his knowledge was not of the brain but of the heart and soul."

Jesus traveled the footpaths and roads of Palestine as the living example of the New Covenant that God had promised many centuries before through the Hebrew prophets. The divine love as perceived through the spiritual vision of Hosea, Jeremiah, Isaiah and Ezekiel had now become a reality in the human heart and was exemplified in all its divine beauty and splendor in Jesus.

Jesus loved all mankind with a love that showed itself in kindness, in service of others, in healing of wounds and sickness, in elevating sorrow and in giving sympathy and comfort. He brought hope and taught redemption to thousands.

It was unfortunate for Spiritualism and the world that Padgett chose to confide in only his closest Spiritualist friends. His decision was influenced because his savings were depleted due to Helen's long illness and he had to continue to work to live. He surely realized that if he revealed his mediumship, it could jeopardize his reputation and law career, so he kept his writing secret for the remainder of his life.

With his passing in 1923, Dr. Stone, his closest friend, became the publisher of his works. Dr. Stone was born in Aldershot, Hampshire, in 1876 and emigrated to Toronto, Canada, in 1903, where he was introduced to Spiritualism. In the fall of 1914 he relocated to Washington, D.C., and became acquainted with James Padgett. Dr. Stone

Leslie R. Stone

was often present during the writing sessions and observed that the spirits' thoughts came in such rapid sweeps of interconnected words that Padgett had no time for thought. In fact, Padgett insisted that he had no clear idea of what his pencil had written until he read it afterwards.

It was a considerable undertaking for Dr. Stone to publish the first book of writings because, with Padgett's style of mediumship, the words were interconnected with-

Example of Padgett's Automatic Writing

out breaks or punctuation. Nevertheless, Dr. Stone persevered and completed his book of "messages" as he called them, in 1940. Unfortunately, by then, Spiritualism in America was a mere shadow of its former self. This was due largely to the successful campaign by the celebrated escape artist Harry Houdini to expose fraud in the seance room. Houdini was successful in turning public opinion against the mediums, which contributed sharply to Spiritualism's decline. This created unfavorable timing for the release of Dr. Stone's book and has contributed to its obscurity.

Although both mediums have passed some time ago, their writings have survived, though not widely known. In them Jesus states, that he wants these teachings made available for all people. It is for this reason that I have published *The Genuine Jesus* to serve as an introduction to the vast legacy of historical, scientific, philosophical and spiritual knowledge received by James E. Padgett and his successor Dr. Daniel G. Samuels.

I hope you enjoy this book and find it thought-provoking and of value on your spiritual journey.

Alan Ross
West Palm Beach, Florida
October 2010

THE
GENUINE
JESUS

A Channeled Autobiography

BIRTH AND YOUTH

Annunciation

I am here to tell you that I am that Jesus of Nazareth who walked the roads of Palestine with my disciples in the days of Herod Antipas and the Roman centurions and the soldiers who filled Jerusalem. My name in Hebrew is Jeshua ben Joseph for I was named after Joshua ben Nun, who followed Moses leading the people to the promised land of Canaan. My mother's name was Miriam, but due to the translation into Latin Miriam became Mary.

My mother told me that the story of the angel coming to her and telling her that she must submit to the birth of a child by the holy spirit, and that as a virgin she would  give birth (Luke 1:31) never took place. The early Christian compilers were seeking something in the Hebrew Scriptures to support their theories of a virgin birth for the Messiah as a means to convert the pagans. A passage was adopted, "Behold, the young woman is with child and will bear a son and will call his name Immanuel" (Isaiah 7:14). This was taken out of context and the Hebrew word "alma" (young woman) was given by the Greek and Latin translators the meaning of virgin. This thought was then expressed as that of a virgin birth for me, so popular among the ancient religions, although Isaiah's prophecy did not refer to me, but to a child born during his time.

Virgin Birth

The concept of the virgin birth was borrowed from ancient legend. I can cite the birth of Horus, an Egyptian, who is said to have been born of a virgin, had his birth announced by an angel and witnessed by shepherds. The earlier Greeks also conceived of gods being born in supernatural ways without the benefit of mortal fathers. Greek legend told of a number of goddesses who gave birth to sons, although they themselves were virgins. I can name such an instance as Danae, who gave birth to Perseus without the benefit of a human mate. She was

supposedly impregnated by Zeus, who came to her in a shower of gold from the sky. It was through the reading of these legends that the idea of making my mother a virgin was secured.

The virgin concept actually dates back to the Buddhist religion. In their writings that deal with the conception of the Buddha, it is described that his mother was transported to a mythical heaven and there impregnated in a mystical way without the benefit of a husband. The writer of the gospel (Luke 1:35) was affected by this story, and, in his desire to give me supernatural status, ascribed to me events analogous to what he found in the writings of these earlier traditions.

Joseph

My father, Joseph, was not a peasant, but a man of considerable spiritual training inasmuch as he held a fine  social position as a descendant of some of the great kings of Israel, notably David and Solomon. He was a devout Jew, a Pharisee at heart, who sought to uphold the Jewish traditions based upon strict observance of Hebrew law. He never supposed at any time that I was not his child, for he was a virile young man and not the decrepit and impotent old man that he has been made out to be. He was legally married to my mother, and their wedding had all the color and pageantry that went with that ancient Hebrew ceremony.

The story of the angel's coming to Joseph and telling him that he must put my mother away because of appearances (Matthew 1:19) is not true. Never in any of my conversations with him did he intimate that such a thing had ever taken place. Furthermore, in later years, a century or so after my death, the idea became popular with the Christian founding fathers to make the world believe that my mother never had any other children. They stated that my brothers James and Jude were my cousins. They invented the story in which my mother, Mary, had a sister by the same name who married the brother of my father, supposedly called Alphaeus. In this way these later writers hoped to induce Christians to believe that my mother had lived as a virgin all her life.

Star of Bethlehem

The Bible account of my birth in Bethlehem is substantially accurate and was the fulfillment of Micah's prophesy (Micah 5:2). My mother gave birth to me in a stable, not because my parents were too poor to afford better lodgings (for my father had a certain amount of money accruing to him through his trade), but because it was census time, and Bethlehem, being a small town had just one inn, and there were no rooms (Luke 2:7).

Two years before my birth a bright star was seen in the eastern sky that caused a great deal of excitement and anxiety in that land. The "Star of Bethlehem", as it is known, was in reality an exploding star, or supernova, which caused a bright light in the sky. The three wise men who saw the star, were astrologers with a knowledge of ancient Chaldean astrological lore and of the Hebrew Scriptures.

They determined that a great event would take place as a result of the appearance of the brilliant light in the heavens. It had been predicted that a king of the Jews was to be born in Judea (Matthew 2:2). The wise men set out for Jerusalem, the capital of Judea, though it was two years before they reached their destination of Jerusalem due to the necessary preparations and the actual journey

crossing the Arabian Desert. The light from the star was no longer with them, having burned out two weeks after it had appeared. They purchased gifts of frankincense and myrrh in addition to a small amount of gold as offerings to me (Matthew 2:11).

Contrary to belief, I was born exactly as other babies are born shortly after midnight on January 7th by the Western calendar. In keeping with tradition, my father celebrated the birth of his first-born by going out into the streets and nearby countryside to look for others who might help him to welcome his newborn son. My father invited some shepherds (Luke 2:15) for wine and cake, and they joined him in offering songs of praise and thanksgiving to God for my safe birth and for my mother's safe delivery. Soon after, I was presented at the Temple in Jerusalem, as was the custom of my people for a newborn (Luke 2:22).

When the wise men reached Jerusalem they first went to the Temple and inquired about the birth of the  one who would be king of the Jews. The high priests sent them to Herod, for they feared that any mention of a Jewish king was political in nature and might be offensive to Herod, with whom they were allied for the maintenance of the status quo in Jerusalem. Herod informed the wise men of rumors that a special birth had taken place in Bethlehem, and he dispatched them to investigate. I was six weeks old when they arrived and they found my birth a humble one, as they had expected (Luke 2:12), and they paid their respects and made their offering to my family.

They did not return to Jerusalem and report to Herod, for they did not want to be responsible for any harm that might come to me. Instead, they departed for their home in the East. When Herod learned that the Magi had disappeared, he took alarm and issued a decree to slaughter all of the infants in the town and its vicinity up to two years of age to be certain to remove any possibility of the appearance of the Jewish redeemer.

Flight to Egypt

Herod's soldiers did not catch me because my father had been quick to realize the possible threat against me. Joseph hastened for us to depart to Egypt using the funds

he had prior to reaching Bethlehem. My mother was able to make the journey, for she had recovered from her lying-in period. Had Herod's edict come earlier, we would not have been able to flee to Egypt because it would have been too soon for my mother to make the journey.

Upon our arrival in Egypt my father sought the home of a relative who lived in Heliopolis, a town not far from Cairo. He welcomed us and enabled us to make a start in this new land. There was quite a community of Jewish people there, and we congregated together for safety as well as for social life. There was a place for worship, a place for the cleansing of women and a school that taught reading and writing to enable youngsters to learn the Scriptures.

My father pursued his occupation as carpenter to support us. In time he was able to establish his trade quite successfully. Our household was a comfortable one with all the conveniences available to a working man of the day. While in Egypt my parents had four other sons and three daughters.

Return to Palestine

As the years passed, my mother became homesick for her people and wanted to return to her native land. My father was hesitant to dismantle the home we had lived in for the past ten years and return to the hazards of travel. He was concerned about safety, not only for me, but for the entire family because conditions in Judea continued to be unsettled even after the death of Herod. The ruler, Archelaus, who followed Herod, continued in his same brutal manner and much blood flowed. There was great unrest and Archelaus, who had been demoted to Ethnarch of Judea, was deposed and sent in exile to Gaul. Still, conditions did not improve much because of the hostility the Jews had for their Roman overlords.

After much hesitation my father and mother decided to break up their home in Egypt and return to the Galilee, and more specifically Nazareth. There was no angel that came to direct my father to make our return (Matthew 2:19).

Growing Up in Nazareth

While growing up in Nazareth, I was a kind and gentle child who loved my mother and father and my brothers and sisters. I was much like other boys with similar feelings, and I engaged in the usual activities of play. The difference was that I did not engage in harmful pranks or naughty deeds, because my soul was constituted to know of God's love and, as a matter of fact, I already had some in my soul.

In school I was taught those things that had to do with the religion of my people, and things that were not religious in nature. I was never taught the philosophy of the Egyptians nor any of the other pagan peoples, and when it is stated that I received my religious ideas or moral teachings from any of these pagan cultures, they are mistaken.

My early life is shrouded in mystery and needs explanation. My education in matters of religion was derived from the teachings of the old Scriptures, or rather from the Jewish teachers who used these texts, and some of the Talmud that was available in my time. My father was very eager for me to fulfill the prophecies and become king of the Jewish nation. He provided me with the funds necessary to learn the Scriptures, which I did with great thoroughness because of my desire to know the things that God had done for us and wanted of my people.

I was a pious student at the synagogue in Nazareth and I held dear the words of my teachers. I studied the Jewish Scriptures and my lessons dealt mainly with the teachings that the prophets of old had  given to the people. In addition, I gained spiritual knowledge and insight directly from my Heavenly Father.

I learned in school of a Messiah who would be a redeemer to my people. This thought clung to me, for some of God's own love was already dwelling in my soul. Throughout my childhood and boyhood I had had constant yearnings for at-onement with God. I believed in the prophecies of Jeremiah and the other prophets that foretold of a Messiah and of a New Heart whereby, God's spirit would be implanted and the stony heart would be removed and replaced with a heart of flesh (Ezekiel 11:19).

I was never in the presence of the Jewish priests at the age of twelve being asked questions or expounding the law to them (Luke 2:42). I was not aware of my mission as Messiah that was yet to come. I never traveled to India, Greece or any other country.

The confusion that has arisen over these alleged stories is due to the fact that throughout the years there have been many Hebrews called Jeshua (Jesus). I can name Jeshua, son of Sirach, in connection with the writings that have been published in the non-canonical books of the Bible. I can also mention that there was a Jeshua who, sometime before my appearance in Palestine, incurred the displeasure of the Jewish authorities and was stoned to death. So you see, in addition to myself, there have been many a mortal called Jeshua and indeed this is a common Hebrew name. No doubt many Hebrews throughout the ages before my time have borne it. Therefore, it is quite possible, and indeed likely, that a man called Jeshua went to the East, studied there and enjoyed the benefit of various philosophies. But I tell you that I never traveled or studied outside of Palestine. I lived at home all the years of my life working hard helping my father with his carpentry trade so that our family could prosper until I started on my public ministry.

Messiah of God

By the time I was twenty, I began to wonder if I might be the promised Messiah prophesied of the Scriptures to

show the people the way to their redemption from their sins. The reality came to me later after frequent communions with God through my spiritual senses. In time I knew from the divine love growing in my soul that the prophecy of the New Heart was being fulfilled within me. I did not have this love in my soul before my birth, but had a predisposition to receive it without conscious knowing.

As time went by, I understood more and more that I needed to become a prophet of the people and not a great military leader such as my ancestor, King David. This was an aspect of my mission that my father was unable to understand. He thought of me as a prophet, as was John the Baptist, one who would appeal to the people to repent of their sins and to be purified of them, and also one who would turn his attention to the sins of the rulers and remind them that Jehovah was Lord and Ruler.

I saw that many of the messianic passages in the books of the prophets could refer to me, for I fulfilled many of the requirements. I was from the house of David (Luke 2:4). I was born in Bethlehem at a time when Judah was a dependency of a foreign power. The prophecies of Daniel also brought the time of the coming of the Messiah to my own days (Daniel 9:25).

When I became convinced of my mission, I tried to tell my family. I told them about my personal relationship with God and of having his divine qualities within my own being. But, according to the religious training and knowledge of my people, such a thing was an utter impossibility, and they thought that I was deranged.

My father was somewhat of a liberal, but he continued to cling to the ideas and beliefs of Hebrew legalisms, the customs and ceremonies so dear to the hearts of the Pharisees. Because of his Jewish training, he was not able to understand my true mission, which was to bring the message that God's divine love was the means to redemption and the bestowal of immortality upon His children.

My father's religious and national outlook caused a divergence between us as I persisted in my belief and later in my conviction that I had been chosen by God for a most high and holy mission. That mission was to bring the glad tidings of the rebestowal of divine love and that it was now available to all those who seek it.

My sisters, Leah and Rachael, wanted nothing to do with my idealism. They were firm in the old traditions of law and Torah. They thought that I possibly could be a zealot leader who would fight Rome, yet they were bewildered because I did not speak belligerently of our enemies, but rather I spoke of peace with them through God's love in man's soul.

THE MINISTRY

John the Baptist

I had known my cousin, John, quite well since my family's return to Palestine from Egypt. John was born in June, six months before me, in the neighborhood of Ain Karim, which is a small town not far from Jerusalem. The story of the angel's coming to announce the birth of John (Luke 1:13) was taken from the story in Genesis of an angel coming to Sarah and telling her that she was to have a son in her old age (Genesis 18:10).

John was the son of Zacharias, a priest who served at the Temple in Jerusalem. John's family was pious and  devout, and filled with a strict interpretation of the law, which the Jews believed had been given to them by Jehovah through Moses. To John's father the laws of Moses represented the most important part of the Jewish religion. He taught John a strict moral code that he absorbed in his youth, which later became the cardinal principles of his brief ministry.

When John was a young man he worked in the wheat fields to earn a livelihood. His true vocation, however, was that of a prophet in the same sense that Elijah was a prophet. That is to say, to tell the rulers and proclaim to the people to repent of their evil ways and to return to the path of righteousness that God had directed the Jews to follow as the great goal of their religion. A religion that called for the love of God and the love of his fellowman.

John was an ascetic who shunned all meat and strong drink. He taught repentance, renunciation of sin and righteousness. He was a great psychic and had visions of who I was and what my mission was to be. Later on, as adults, we discussed the way I should be revealed to our people. It was decided that John would be the forerunner and prepare the way for my coming (Matthew 11:10). This meant that he would preach in various places ahead of me so that, when I arrived, the people's curiosity would be aroused to know who I was.

John began his ministry a few months before mine when he preached along the banks of the Jordan to those

Judeans who would gather to hear him. We never preached together in the same place, for that would have defeated the purpose of his mission to straighten the path for my coming (Matthew 3:3).

He never tried to lead a reform movement independent of me, nor was he influenced by the Essenes, whose views of purity led them to live away from the contaminations of civilization in isolated communities where they carried out their religious practices. For, like John, I believed not in retreat from the world but in carrying the message of God out to the people. John realized the differences in our missions and spoke of his not being worthy to unloosen my shoes (Mark 1:7).

My ministry was worked out between us and was part of a prearranged plan. Thus, the gospel is not true that declares that John did not know me but would anoint the one on whom a dove would descend (John 1:32-33). He anointed me not because of any dove or a voice from heaven, but because he was convinced in his heart that I was the promised Messiah of the old Scriptures.

I was baptized by stepping into the River Jordan waist deep and, with the waters cupped in his hands, John poured the water upon my head in the symbolic act of coronation, as the old Hebrew priests anointed the kings of Israel and Judah. I became the Christ at that moment because I was also anointed by my Heavenly Father, filling my soul with his own substance and essence. A voice from the realm of spirit was heard saying, "This is my beloved son in whom I am well pleased" (Matthew 3:17).

The Christian concept of baptism by water eventually superseded the ancient Hebrew custom of sacrifice and became the rite of dedication. Thus, just as I had been baptized in water by John, baptism eventually became the religious symbol of regeneration for Christian salvation.

The baptism of infants has no virtue to save them from their sins or to make them at-one with God. The mere fact that water is sprinkled on an infant's head and some blessing pronounced by a preacher does not in any way bring that infant into unison with God.

Baptism is man's creation and means nothing more to God than an outward ceremony that affects the infant

in regard to its connection with the established earthly church. In no way does it have any effect upon the soul of the infant. The tendency of this ceremony is to make people neglectful of the great truth, that it is their own efforts that will bring them into harmony with God's laws of love and redemption.

John was a true prophet, for he not only preached repentance to all who would listen, but he also thundered against what he considered the evil conduct of Herod for transgressions against God's law of matrimony. John looked upon Herod's marriage to Herodias as illegal (Mark 6:18), an act that could bring upon his subjects the wrath of God. The Pharisees, to whom John belonged, believed their marriage was not legal because no woman, as it was understood, could contract marriage with the brother of a deceased husband when children had been born of the first marriage. Hence Salome, the offspring of Herodias and Herod's stepbrother, invalidated this marriage to Herod. It was this violation of our levirate marriage law that prompted John's preaching against him.

It is true, of course, that Herodias was incensed against John for, as a member of the ruling class, she was at heart a Sadducee and did not believe in the correctness of his views. She therefore was elated to see him imprisoned and silenced. Herod did not concern himself that much about this part of John's preaching. While he disagreed with his interpretation of the marriage law, wrangling between the Pharisees and the Sadducees had been going on for two centuries, and such legalistic disputes did not have the urgency for Herod as this particular one had for Herodias. He was concerned rather with the attitude the Roman overlords would take towards religious gatherings that could be a pretext for sedition and rebellion. He thought it wise to arrest John who could be the possible cause of disorder in his territory.

Although John was not preaching where he was subject to Herod's jurisdiction, he sent soldiers in the garb of travelers to seek John out without arousing suspicion. John was sequestered into Herod's land and taken to the fortress of Macherus near the Dead Sea. He was confined there for about ten months, or until Herod's birthday. Herod was not anxious for John's death, but Herodias wanted it and her request was granted.

Salome did dance at this festival (Mark 6:22), but it is not true that her dancing made Herod grant her request for John's death. She never asked for John's decapitation, and I can state for a fact that his head was never brought in before the king on a platter (Matthew 14:8). These are fanciful ideas that students of the old writings used to associate me with the story of the festival of Purim when King Ahasuerus vowed to grant Esther anything she asked for if she would dance for him at his banquet (Esther 5:6).

Christ

The Jews expected a Messiah who would lead the people to victory over the Romans in warfare and free their country from foreign rule, but there was no unanimity about who and what the Messiah would be. There were those who thought that being sent by God, he  would live forever in the flesh. Such was the ignorance of the Jews of things spiritual and their utter carnality of mind that all their religious and spiritual speculations and aspirations were centered upon the material. They could not understand that the christ meant the christ principle, or the very essence of God, which is divine love.

I became the Christ at the time of my baptism, when the holy spirit descended upon me with a great inflowing of divine love. It entered my soul and transformed it from the image of God, as it was created, into the actual substance and essence of God that it had now become. My human soul was now a divine soul with all the attributes of God's divine nature. This is the true meaning of the word "christ", as it is generally used, referring to the anointed one or the saviour.

Christ then is actually the principle of God's love that was first made available as it appeared in my soul when I proclaimed my mission on earth. It is this love that saves when it enters the soul of the mortal or spirit. No blood on the cross or any mysterious sacrament of bread and wine will achieve salvation and at-onement with God, only divine love has the power to cause the errors and evils of the human soul to disappear and thus give a New Heart free of sin.

Then, having christ in you means having divine love dwelling in your soul. If you read the epistle of John, the apostle, you will understand the truth of the saying that the kingdom of God is within you. For I said, "Herein is love, not that we loved God, but that he loved us" (1 John 4:10). "God is love, and he that dwelleth in this love dwelleth in God and God in him" (1 John 1:16). John made it clear that when he spoke of love, he meant God's love for all mankind, and where this love is, there will be God in spirit.

When I said, "Where two or three are gathered together in my name, there I will be also" (Matthew 18:20), I did not mean that I would be there in person, for this would be impossible. As an individualized spirit, I am limited in my place of occupancy and cannot be in sev-

eral places at once; but christ can. What I meant was that where two or three are gathered together for the purpose of seeking God's divine love, I would be able to help them feel its influence. I would not need to be present for that purpose, for I would be represented by the holy spirit. This means that, as the Christ, I would be with all souls whenever they seek my help to receive this principle.

Now the expression, "son of man", applies to me in various places in the New Testament and has a special meaning connected with my messiahship. The term conceived by Ezekiel meant not merely man as a living being, but man the creation of God, and therefore son of man meant God's specially created being with whom he could communicate concerning his affairs. Hence, "son of man" meant a prophet who could be God's spokesman (Ezekiel 2:1). When I came to deliver my message proclaiming the availability of God's divine love, I considered myself to be the "son of man" as the prophet of Jehovah at the time. In fact, God's love already dwelt in my soul to a considerable degree, and I knew what he wanted of me and I strove to carry out his wishes (John 8:29).

I never said that I was God, nor did I ever create any part of the universe. I am merely a spirit sent by God to lead men to redemption and to show them the way to the heavenly home that has been prepared for those who pray for God's love.

Wilderness and Temptation

I never entered the desert between Jerusalem and the Dead Sea as has been written, nor did I fast for forty days and forty nights. I did not believe in fasting as a cure for sin. The only fasting I believed in was the fasting of the soul from its desire to act in a way contrary to the laws of God. I was never tempted by the devil, because there is no devil or Satan (Matthew 4:1).

It was the early writers who conceived the figure of a disobedient archangel who warred against God and was thrown out of heaven to become the prince of darkness, master of the earth. To this archangel they gave the name Lucifer and endowed him with the ability to change his form; and he was cursed by God and became a serpent. Thus, the myth was born that the serpent was symbolic of the prince of darkness, or Satan (Revelation 12:9).

There is no such thing as fallen angels who, through ambition or any other reason, revolted against the power of God's government and thereby lost their estate as angels. Never was there any Lucifer and never were there any angels thrown from the battlements of heaven into hell. This temptation story was inspired from the  Buddha stories. It was taken from the account of the Buddha withstanding the temptations of the powers of the prince of evil, whose attacks against the person of the Buddha were frustrated by his holiness.

I never said, as indicated in the distorted writings of the gospel of John, that the Jews were born of the devil and were descendants of a murderer or murderess and had cut themselves off from God (John 8:44), nor did I call the Jews "children of Satan". There were some things I did not come to preach, and hatred against man or nation was one of them. This passage has caused a great deal of anger and hatred to be directed against the Jews for their obstinacy in not accepting me as their long-awaited-for Messiah.

Proclaimed Messiahship

The one sign that I waited for was the desecration of the Temple, prophesied in the old writings. (Daniel 8:14). When Pontius Pilate began his rule early in A.D. 26, he committed, as one of his first acts, the dastardly deed of desecration of the Temple. Pilate ordered his soldiers to enter therein with their idolatrous standards and banners. I knew then that I must come forth and proclaim that I had been anointed the Messiah of God.

I began my public ministry at the age of thirty-three.  I did not come to bring something new and revolutionary, but rather I came as the fulfillment of the Scriptures. I never entertained the idea of establishing a new religion; for the religion of God had already been established within Judaism.

As a religious Jew, I was intent upon living up to the highest ideals of Judaism in the way of the ethical standard of life as preached by our prophets and lawgivers. I was wholeheartedly attached to my own religious institution, the Temple at Jerusalem, and the assemblies and synagogues of Judaism. I planned to work strictly with the established Hebrew church to effect needed reforms from within as well as to introduce the christ principle to my people.

When the time was right, I proclaimed my messiahship to the entire congregation at the synagogue in Nazareth (Luke 4:16). Of course, it created a sensation when I read "The spirit of Jehovah is upon me and has anointed me to proclaim the glad tidings" (Luke 4:18). What I meant was that God had appointed me to preach the re-bestowal of his divine love, which had been made a reality in my own soul.

I also declared to the listeners in the synagogue, "Today is this Scripture fulfilled in your ears" (Luke 4:21). Though the main body of my sermon was based on the sixty-first chapter of Isaiah. When I recited this passage on the delivery of the captives (Isaiah 61:1), what I meant was freedom delivered from sin not through adherence to the Mosaic law alone, which was all that was available before my coming, but through the efficacy of God's divine love.

Having lived in Nazareth for twenty-three years, the people who knew me for so long were now suddenly expected to believe that I was the promised Messiah of the Scriptures. This was very difficult for them since I had never healed before in Nazareth, and the people were skeptical whether I could suddenly perform what I had never done before. There was a strong current of incredulity that prevented me from exercising  my healing powers, because faith on the part of the recipient is required to heal. Therefore, it is true that I was unable to perform any miracles at that time (Matthew 13:58) because of these particular circumstances.

My mother loved me very much and was fearful of my mission, in that I might bring down upon me the opposition of the Jewish authorities as well as the Roman legions. On occasion she accompanied me to see that no harm would come to me. One time she came with some of my brothers and sisters to urge me to give up my mission and come back to Nazareth and lead a quiet life with marriage and a family of my own. They wanted me to forget that I should be king of the Jews either in a spiritual sense or in a purely material one. However, their plea was to no avail because, having been anointed the Christ, I was compelled to begin my mission preaching to all those who would hear the way to end sin and sickness and to inherit the kingdom of God.

Condition of the World

When I came to teach the truths of my Heavenly Father, the Hebrew nation was struggling under the tyranny of the Roman Empire. The barbarism practiced by the pagan conquerors, in addition to the cruelties evoked by the Hebrew rulers, placed an unrelenting, heartless yoke of oppression upon the Jews and their way of life.

The group of Palestinian Jews known as the Pharisees

was composed of the common people, the artisans and the tradesmen. They were downtrodden by the Sadducees, the rich aristocrats. They were the ruling class, an elitist group who cared nothing for the Scriptures except as their own interests were concerned. These two religious parties disagreed frequently over the interpretation of the oral law, which was the Hebrew code of the unwritten interpretations of the Mosaic law.

The Pharisees were deeply concerned with the immortality of the soul, inasmuch as their own plight on earth made them seek for justice in an ideal world beyond the grave. They felt that God's righteousness embraced a kingdom where justice and mercy would be the established order. That is why the Pharisees were willing to listen to me, yet they were not fully able to understand the principle I taught that divine love was the way to spiritual rebirth.

For centuries the Pharisees had battled stubbornly against the Sadducees' denial of immortality of the soul. The Sadducees had clung to their faith upon entering the Hebrew paradise through the keeping of the Commandments and the studying of the Torah. In their decrees, precepts and interpretations that stemmed from these sacred works, the divine love was alien to their fundamental concept of religion, which is what prevented them from accepting me as the Messiah.

At this time the world was nearly completely devoid of the spiritual conception of the true relationship between God and man. God was a being of anger and wrath only, and because of this concept, the Jews were devoid of the knowledge of God's nature of goodness and mercy. The only God they knew was interested in their material welfare, and they did not realize that God wanted them to know him as their spiritual Father.

When I came, they looked upon me, that is, those Jews who accepted me as their Messiah, as the one who would liberate them from the oppression that their

Roman conquerors had placed upon them. They thought that I would make them a great and independent nation, more powerful than all the other nations and fit to rule the world. No, this is all wrong, and could not happen, for God is not the God of any nation or race and, as such, will not help any nation commit acts of aggression to gain victory over another. God will, however, respond to every individual who comes to him in true supplication seeking his help.

The Jews had no conception of my true mission nor what the divine love actually meant. The one who had the most approximate knowledge of it was Mary

Magdalene because of a certain predisposition of her soul. John had a realization of what my coming meant, and that was because of the great love that was a part of his nature. My other disciples, until shortly before my death, looked upon me only as a saviour from their burdens that the Roman yoke had placed upon them.

I explained my mission to John and taught him the spiritual truths that I had come to teach, that is, the way to the kingdom of immortal souls. Hence, only in John's gospel is written the necessary requirement for full salvation—I mean, the declaration that "You must be born again in order to enter into the kingdom of God" (John 3:3). This is the true way by which one can become a child of God and be fit to live in and enjoy the kingdom of heaven.

First Disciples

My first disciples were comparatively ignorant men, fishermen by occupation, who had no education above  the ordinary workman of the time. When I called upon them to become my disciples (Mark 1:17), they were surprised and hesitated.

The knowledge they gained during our time together came from their faith in the great truths that I had taught them, and, in their observation of the great power that I displayed and in the great love that I possessed. My first disciples were quite different in their individual personalities and temperament, although they were united with me throughout our travels during the execution of my mission in Palestine.

They were the recipients of my daily instructions, advice and encouragement. Despite all the perplexities and divergences of thoughts, ambitions and degrees of faith on the part of my first disciples, I was able to weld them into a very capable group of men devoted to the cause of bringing the kingdom of God to human possession.

Any religious differences among them or any disputes of a personal nature were settled by me amicably and not in a formal manner, but informally as befitted the men who followed me. This was without recourse to the legal and technical formulas presented by the churches of the day. My disciples saw that prayer to God brings humility, forbearance and forgiveness and, if one does this, it will show that the divine love is present in his soul. Prayer to God causes this love to flow into the soul and in time it displaces, or causes to displace, suspicion, judgement, jealousies and competition.

My first disciples needed divine love to have a common bond for a soul relationship among them. Peter first understood this in a physical way and thought I was referring to baptism, which was not the case. He thought this because I used water to implement my teachings of God's love, which was something that my disciples could understand. I also used many other illustrations in addition to water, such as the bread, the new cloth, and the new wine.

Philip and Nathaniel both proclaimed me to be the Messiah, that is to say, the son of God or Redeemer. Andrew was the one who told Peter that he had met the Messiah, and thus Peter came to meet me, but he was not the first to make this announcement. Peter possessed more love than the other disciples, except for John.

John was a man of a very affectionate nature and was with me a great deal during my ministry. Although he was not what was called a learned man, he was acquainted with the philosophies of the prophets of the old Scriptures. I selected John to become one of my disciples because of his susceptibility to my teachings and the possibility for developing his spiritual nature.

Peter understood that I was the true son of the living God (John 6:69), but he never declared that I was God. He was a man filled with zeal and ambition, but his development of love was not sufficient to enable him to realize fully that my kingdom was not an earthly one, but was one high up in the spirit world. After my death Peter gained conviction in my teachings in all their truth and fullness, and he became the most powerful and influential of all my disciples.

Nicodemus

When I was teaching in Palestine, I had a meeting with Nicodemus, the son of Gurion the Pharisee.  Nicodemus' father was a rabbi who held religious discussion groups, as was the custom of the day. Nicodemus wanted to know about the kingdom of God and how to enter therein. Since he was not able to understand fully my meaning, he came one evening to hear in private what he had only been able to get a glimpse of at my public sermons in the marketplace.

To his query I showed that being born of the flesh was the work of the womb, and that in this sense there was no possibility of rebirth, but spiritually the soul could be reborn through prayer. Nicodemus had difficulty understanding what I meant by the transformation of the soul from the human into the divine, so I had recourse to use a parable as I usually had in speaking to the people, "Except a man be born again, he cannot seek the kingdom of God" (John 3:3).

Nicodemus could not understand a spiritual rebirth, but he could understand the following of the moral code by doing good deeds, practicing mercy and charity, righteous conduct and pity for the widow and the orphan. In short, he understood repentance from sin in a prophetic sense, which he believed gave immortality to the soul and earned it entrance into the kingdom. I explained to him that the practicing of these virtues purifies the soul and makes it a perfect human soul in the eyes of God, but to enter the kingdom, the soul has to be transformed into a divine soul through God's nature—divine love.

Divine love is what renders the soul immortal and enables it to enter the kingdom of God, and not the perfection of the human soul that results from the doing of good deeds and the practicing of charity and righteousness.

Sermon on the Mount

Not all the sayings and blessings attributed to the Sermon on the Mount were given by me at one particular time as recorded in the gospel (Matthew 5). Instead, they are the result of a great number of  sermons dealing with the spiritual lives of the Jews who lived at the time. They were compiled by the gospel copyists in the form of a synopsis to cover a considerable vista of my spiritual discourses. Much of what I said pertained to the development of the human or natural love because this was the only love known to the Jews at the time. These sermons dealt with the development of this love as found in the moral code and the exhortations of the old writings that could be understood by my hearers. I used these teachings as a bridge to lead to the unknown subject of the divine love and the rebirth that it brings.

In the gospels there are a number of blessings that I never used at all, and others that were the subjects of considerable sermons rather than the brief blessings that survived to be recorded. I did say, "Blessed are the poor in spirit" (Matthew 5:3). By this, I meant that those of spiritual lack, and who realized it, were blessed because this knowledge or intuition of their lack would turn them either to follow God's laws and obtain spiritual development in that way, or to seek divine love and obtain soul development in that way.

I also blessed the people, who listened to me because of their gentleness or meekness, for I said that they would inherit the land (Matthew 5:5). What I meant by this was that violence and quarrels and wars were sinful in the eyes of God, and keeping from these offenses would enable men to come into harmony and eventually reach the spiritual heaven of purified souls. I taught that gentility of heart could now be obtained through God's love that would not merely purify the soul but transform it so that the sins of vengeance, hatred, corruption and murder would cease to be encrustations of that soul. The resultant gentility of heart would fit that soul for a wonderful spiritual home. This is what I meant by "The meek shall inherit the earth" (Matthew 5:5). I did not mean the material earth but the promised land in heaven of the New Jerusalem; and not for the material body, but for the soul in its spirit body transformed into a divine angel.

I said, "Blessed are they that mourn, for they shall be comforted" (Matthew 5:4). What I meant by this was that there would be more than the mere religious consolation for the bereaved who are saddened by the death of a loved one. But those who have had a loss can have faith that God's spiritual universe is populated with the souls of those who have left the earth forever. These spirits are alive and working out their progress towards happiness that could never be achieved on earth. The grave simply took their envelope of flesh. So you see, their dear departed are still alive and they will be with them again at some time in the future. This was the comfort I spoke of for the Hebrew people, who had a very limited understanding of the spiritual aspects of life after death.

I blessed the people, saying, "Blessed are the pure in heart, for they shall see God" (Matthew 5:8). I did not literally mean that they will see God, for this would be impossible. What I meant was that those who had achieved the paradise of the Hebrews by their purity of heart could gain God's love and the soul development to see God in all of His beauty. I do not mean that the possessor of divine love will actually see God in form or feature, but what I meant was that his soul perceptions would be opened and in such a condition that all the attributes of God will appear vividly to his inner senses and will seem as real as anything that can be seen with our spirit vision.

Thus, the blessings had a spiritual as well as a soul aspect, and those who could not understand the divine love could understand the blessings as they pertained to the human or natural love.

Healing

I healed the sick, the deaf, the withered hand of the palsied man and the blind man at the pool of Siloam: he was cured because of his faith (John 9:7) in me and in my powers as the Messiah.

There was a Gentile woman who sought me out to have me cure her sick daughter. She addressed me as rabbi, for she knew I was of the Jewish nation. I told her to approach, although some of my eager disciples wished to chase her away, but I wouldn't hear of it, and because of her faith I was able to heal her daughter (Matthew 15:22-23).

Healing is effected as a result of rapport between the mortal doctor or healer and the spirit healers who are transmitting those therapeutic forces to the ailing person. The mortal healer through his spiritual condition can attract the spirit healers; however, if the ailing person can lift him or herself above the earth plane through faith and prayer, the spirit healer can work directly with the patient to accomplish the healing. In either case divine love is not necessary to effect the healing.

What is required is faith that God will help and that the healing forces of the spiritual world will be set in motion. The spirit healers can also put the patient in a condition by which evil spirits, who can intensify the distress or cause it to persist, are separated from their contact and control of the patient to allow the healers to do their work without hindrance. All of the ministering angels who do this work once inhabited a physical body and, as such, have the sympathy that enables them to understand the suffering of the mortal world.

The prayers and faith of a loved one for a sick person are of great benefit. Often the best physicians are those who, in earnestness of love and sympathy, send their prayers to God in faith that He will accomplish what mortal medicine cannot. Although there are times when, despite sincere prayer, the death of a loved one does occur. This is due to the fact that aside from the spiritual forces engaged, the healing process depends upon the condition of the organ to be restored.

An organ that is in good functioning order can be restored to perfect health regardless of the pathological disturbance from which it may suffer. But an organ that has reached a condition of irreversible weakness or malfunction through misuse or old age cannot be healed or restored. Deterioration of the physical body is natural due to aging. Then comes the time for that person to relinquish his tired, worn-out body and enter upon a new life in the spirit world in its spirit body.

Lazarus

I wish to explain my visit to the house of Lazarus and my healing him of his uncon- scious condition, which actu- ally was a coma, a state not known to the people at the time, that has erroneously been described as being dead by the gospel writers (John 12:1).

They were wrong in this, for I did not say this sick- ness is not unto death but, for the glory of God, the son might be glorified (John 11:4). This meant that his sick- ness would not end in his death because I would raise him from the dead. This, however, was not the case. What I did say was, "This sickness is not unto death, for through the power of God, the son will heal him and be glorified." What this meant was that I would show that I had come to heal Lazarus and had been given the power by God to cure him of his illness.

Furthermore, I did say, as recorded, "Our friend Lazarus sleepeth; but I go, that I may awaken him out of his sleep" (John 11:11). Now, the gospel of John, which at this point was not written by John, declares that by "sleep" I meant death, but this is not true. Had I meant that Lazarus was dead, I would have used one of the expressions that were common at the time to indicate that. These were "to sleep with one's Father" or "to sleep in the dust" or "to be in perpetual sleep." Hence, when I said, "Lazarus was asleep," I meant that he was in that unconscious state in which one is dying in one's sleep. When I wept, and it is true, for I did weep (John 11:35), it was because I was touched with emotion by the restoration of the life of a man I loved.

I also wish to explain an expression that, if not correctly understood, tends to give the impression of cruelty and indifference to human suffering. I never advocated or taught mutilation of the body, in any form such as the saying attributed to me in the gospels, "If thy right eye offend thee, pluck it out and cast it from thee, for it is profitable for thee that one of thy members should perish and not that thy whole body be cast into hell" (Matthew 5:29). This does not give the true meaning of my saying, for I meant that the eye reflects the state of the soul, and of the emotions. So, if the eye reveals a wicked emotion, it means the soul is possessed of wickedness and, by plucking out the eye, I simply meant to pluck out the evil emotion from the soul.

In the same way my reference to the cutting off the hand that offends (Matthew 5:30) did not refer literally to the physical hand, but to the action performed by the hand resulting from a sinful soul. I simply meant eradication of the evil emotion in the soul that produced an evil action.

The physical plucking out of an eye or the cutting off of a limb could have no effect on the soul to free it from sin, for it is not the body but the soul that is sinful; the body simply carries out the desires of the soul. Such mutilations could not have any effect upon the soul in the way of eliminating sin. Sin is eliminated through the will and the feeling of remorse that change the soul's condition and cause it to turn to God in earnest prayer for forgiveness.

Transfiguration

At the time of my birth, divine love was bestowed to mortals and spirits alike. Spirits living in the higher realms came to receive this gift and became partakers of this love and the possessors of immortality.

Thus, at the time of the Transfiguration on the Mount, Moses and Elijah were the leaders of this group  of spirits who had obtained their portions of divine love. The appearance of the three of us together on the mount was to show that this love had been bestowed and received by me and those deserving spirits. Moses and Elijah had this love to such an extent that the three of us standing there together were all shining and bright.

Peter, John and James accompanied me to the Mount and witnessed the event. They fell to their faces because of the exceeding brightness of our combined countenance. The voice they heard saying, "Hear ye him," which proclaimed that I was the well-beloved son (Luke 9:35), was not the voice of God, but of an angel whose mission it was to make this proclamation.

I never said, "But I say unto you Elijah is come" (Matthew 17:12). What I did say was, "But I say unto you that one like Elijah has come". I did refer to John the Baptist who, in his type of sermon, his temperament, and even his garb and food, was a throwback to Elijah. Here the similarity ended, for each of these men lived different lives and are individual spirits, both living in the kingdom of God at the same time.

Greater Works

"Verily, verily, I say unto you, he that believeth in me, the works that I do shall he do also and greater works than these shall he do, because I go unto my Father" (John 14:12). What I meant by "works", are those things that the world considered as miracles. I assured my disciples that they would have the power to do similar works or perform similar miracles and to a greater extent than I had performed them. When I said this to them what I meant was that during their ministries as a group they would be able to perform a greater number of miracles than I had, however greater meant in quantity, not in quality.

This power, or the successful exercise of it, was not dependent upon belief in my name, but upon their faith in the power of God, and in the fact that this power would be conferred upon them. There is no virtue in my name or in me as the individual Jesus, but all virtue rests in the faith that they might have in the Father. I never performed any of the miracles of my own, but were all performed by God working through me. Just as this power worked through me, it would work through them when they acquired the necessary faith.

The Biblical expression, "And whatsoever ye shall ask in my name, that will I do, that the Father may be glorified in the son" (John 14:13). The belief that my name is sufficient to cause the workings of miracles is all wrong. I never said that such belief was what was required. Neither did I say, "Whatsoever should be asked of the Father in my name would be given to men" (John 15:16). This is all wrong, for I am not a part of the Godhead, and my name does not have any miraculous influence with God.

I am a man as other men are men. The only difference is that my soul was created to fulfill the Scriptures by becoming one with God's love to give me my spiritual powers. Thus, I had knowledge of the laws that enabled me to bring into operation those forces that would cause the desired effects to appear as realities to the people. Belief in my name does not cause the working of these laws or their response regardless of the sincerity of the supplication.

All acts that are apparently miracles are controlled by laws just as the forces that mortals call the workings of nature are controlled by laws. When sufficient faith is acquired, there comes to its possessor knowledge of these laws. This faith may not be perceptible to the ordinary physical senses, but instead to the inner senses of the soul that enables comprehension of the things spiritual. With knowledge of the inner senses these laws may be controlled so that the effects that they bring about appear to be contrary to the accustomed workings of the laws of nature and appear as miracles.

Until my disciples had acquired the sufficient faith that brought this knowledge to their inner senses, they could not perform any miracles.

Miracles

At the marriage feast at Cana (John 2:1), a so-called miracle that needs clarification, is my supposed changing of water to wine. A cousin of mine on my mother's side of the family was being married and, as the wine ran out, I was able to procure some from a nearby wine dealer by simply paying for it, and I used water jugs to carry it back to the wedding party. The New Testament story of the miraculous changing of water to wine was actually borrowed from the Greek account of Dionysius of Elis, the god of wine. Legend has it that he would place jars of water in a concealed chamber overnight, and the next morning they would be turned to wine.

When news arrived of my cousin John's death, I retreated to a remote place in the hills of Trans-Jordan to pray. When I came out, I was met by a great multitude of people and was moved with compassion for them and healed their sick.

It was meal time and the people were hungry. Those who ate supper with me had bread and fish and wine (Matthew 14:17), and we even had figs and dates, which the New Testament does not mention. I did not create this food in  some miraculous way, even though I had wonderful powers and understood the workings of the spiritual laws to a far greater extent than any mortal who had ever lived. Despite this, I had not the power to increase the loaves and fishes, as is set forth in the account of the miracle. To be able to do so would go against the laws of God that govern the material things of creation and would be beyond the powers conferred on me or any mortal or spirit.

The food had either been brought along by the people or, in the case of the fish, they had been caught by my disciples. Though, it is true that I did tell them where to cast their nets to be able to make a great haul of fish (John 21:6), which they did. This took place as a result of my psychic knowledge that a large school of fish had just reached that part of the lake. The incident that the New Testament compilers adopted to represent me to as having fed five thousand came from the story in which Elisha feeds one hundred men with only the first fruits of some corn and bread (2 Kings 4:42).

That evening my disciples took their fishing boat and turned back to Galilee in the vicinity of Capernaum. I remained behind to dismiss the multitude, which was not four or five thousand but considerably less, and then I withdrew to pray.

Later I took one of the many little boats that were anchored along the shore and I made my way in it. As the wind was strong, I was able to catch up with my disciples, who were happy to see me and took me into their fishing boat. The sea was rough and they were frightened (Matthew 14:24). Peter told me to stand up by the mast so the men could see me and gain faith and courage. The moonlight was shining on my white robe and it appeared, as later told, that I looked like a ghost, and from the shore it seemed as though I were walking on the

waves (Matthew 14:26). The later New Testament compilers turned to tales in Greek mythology regarding this event, and in a similar way they read that Poseidon, the god of the sea, walked on water, and this was sufficient for them to imagine me having done the same.

Now regarding my casting out of evil spirits, the incident of the swine was not recorded accurately (Matthew 8:31-32). I had no authority to permit the evil spirits to enter into the swine. The result would be that the property of the innocent owner would have been taken from him and lost. To allow the swine to receive these spirits and thereby perish would not have been in consonance with my love and idea of what was just.

All of the instances of alleged miracles attributed to me by the New Testament writers were not done with any malicious intent, but with the desire to stress my supernatural powers to the point of making me a divinity equal to that of God. The aim of those in power was to institutionalize Christianity and keep their power by making their priestly class and its functions the dominant part of the religion. In this way the Roman Church eventually fell into the same pit of ambition and worldliness that the Jewish people had accused the Sanhedrin of doing.

Institutionalized Christianity perpetuated a system entirely man-made that lacked the essential of spirituality—divine love. It is this love that was the paramount reason for my ministry and the cornerstone of my teachings.

Good Shepherd

When on earth I never said that I was the Good Shepherd (John 10:11), for this referred to my Heavenly Father. This statement was inserted many years after my death in order to raise me up to be co-equal with God. What I did say was that God is the Good Shepherd and the sheepfold is the kingdom of heaven, and that I was the door

(John 10:9) through which the sheep came into the fold and into the presence and knowledge of the Good Shepherd. God gives life, and I am the way, and the gate through which the sheep may enter the sheepfold of eternal life (John 10:7). In the Psalms it is pointed out that the Good Shepherd, God, would use King David, or better, a root of David as a helper to bring the sheep into the fold.

One of the best known Psalms is the twenty-third written by David, which I used in my teachings to show  the distinction between the old teachings and the new ones I gave to the people. In this psalm, God is described as a Shepherd who leads the flock beside the still waters and to lie down in green pastures (Psalms 23:2). This psalm can be interpreted as nostalgia for the countryside and its tranquility away from the cares and vexations of city life, with a longing to be alone in God's creation to commune with him and purify one's heart. This psalm actually has a more spiritual meaning and is really a description of the kingdom of heaven, for such things are there to make the spirit happy in its celestial home.

This psalm gives to the people an understanding that death does not mean the cessation of the conscious human personality, for the psalm mentions, "Yea, though I pass through the valley of the shadow of death, I shall fear no evil, for Thou art with me; Thy rod and Thy staff, they comfort me" (Psalms 23:4). This picture that I made was one that the people could understand. It was of a God who would care for the troubled soul entering the spirit world, and faith would enable the ministering angels to help that soul progress to a place where it would eventually find the peace and happiness of the still waters and the green pastures.

The psalm describes this by the means of a feast for the soul; "Thou preparest a table before me in the presence of mine enemies; thou anointest my head with oil; my cup runneth over" (Psalms 23:5). Here I expressed that the soul with divine love will eliminate all thoughts of vengeance, or overcoming enemies, and will entertain only sentiments of love for his fellowman.

When I recited the psalm, "And I shall dwell in the house of the Lord forever" (Psalms 23:6), I simply meant that life in the paradise of the Hebrews has no certainty of immortality, whereas the soul possessed of divine love has a consciousness of its immortality and will live for all eternity. I used many psalms and other passages from the Hebrew Scriptures to show the greater glory that comes to those who are the possessors of God's love.

THE LAST WEEK

Entry into Jerusalem

Isaiah was positive that the word of God must come from Jerusalem (Isaiah 2:3). I believed this too, which is the reason I went to Jerusalem to bring the message of God to the city of David.

When my disciples and I approached Jerusalem at Bethphage near the Mount of Olives, I sent two of them ahead telling them to go to the village visible in the distance and bring to me the ass and her colt that they would  find tied there. I told them that if anyone questions why you want them, explain to them that they are for your Master who needs them for the Lord's work, and they will let you take them (Matthew 21:2-3). This was the fulfillment of the prophecy, "Behold, Jerusalem! Your king will come riding humbly on a colt, the foal of an ass!" (Zechariah 9:9).

My disciples went forth and carried out my instructions. They returned with the animals and put cloaks over their backs, and I got up upon the colt. When I entered the city, many people put their cloaks on the ground while others cut palm branches and laid them along the path. The crowd that preceded me and those who followed praised me saying; "God bless the descendent of David, he who comes in the name of the Lord" (Matthew 21:9). The people were excited. Some asked who I was; others answered, "This is the saviour, the promised Messiah, Jesus of Nazareth" (Matthew 21:11).

Zechariah knew through his inner senses that the Messiah must be a human being possessed of the transcendental spiritual qualities of love and humility. In addition, he saw that the Messiah would not only have Israel at heart but all nations. He would bring peace to the war-torn world through his care, his love and his mercy. I was very impressed by the verses of Zechariah, and in my soul I knew that his concept of the Messiah was in accord with what God had determined for his Christ. So when I set out for Jerusalem, I chose to enter the city exactly in the manner described by Zechariah.

Cleansing the Temple

When I saw the merchants in the Temple courtyard, I said to them "God's house shall be called the house of  prayer; but ye have made it a den of thieves" (Matthew 21:13). I entered with a piece of rope in which I had tied knots and, as I swung it about, the many animals in the courtyard to be sold as sacrifice for the Passover stampeded, overturning the tables, and scattering the wares. Afterward, I healed the blind and the lame who came to me at the Temple.

The sacrifice of animals performed by the priests was a pagan concept and a practice that Abraham, enlightened by God, had abandoned. However, it was consistent with the priesthood's plan to perform it as a religious function of a national nature. These sacrifices enabled the priesthood to live, for they had difficulties in making ends meet because the people were not so generous in their contributions to the Temple.

The story of Abraham binding his son, Isaac, to an

altar stone and the latter being saved by an angel from sacrifice (Genesis 22:11-12) is not a narrative depicting the true test of Abraham's faith in the Lord, as the Bible commentators mistakenly think.

Abraham's faith in God had been put to the test repeatedly by the rigors and hardships that he had faced and borne for months in the slow arduous trek from his native Ur, in his old age, to a new life at the call of a God he could not see, but in his heart he knew was the living king of the universe. The saving of Isaac was not a test at all, but undeniable proof with the stamp of God that those who worship him be in truth to the statutes of righteousness, justice and mercy.

The Pharisees came to me with a woman taken in adultery. They came to test my judgement to see in what way my decision would differ from that of Moses. The New Testament states, "This they said, tempting him, that they might have something with which to accuse him" (John 8:6). If I had declared against stoning the woman, they would accuse me of breaking the Mosaic law, and if I had upheld the law, they were going to accuse me of being inhuman, which was inconsistent with God's forgiveness and mercy and would prove me to be an imposter.

The gospel of John does not mention their motives, but I knew what was on their minds and I made my decision as John recorded it, "He that is without sin among you, let him first cast a stone at her" (John 8:7)

Fig Tree

I left Jerusalem and went to the city of Bethany and lodged there for the night (Matthew 21:17). When I returned to Jerusalem, it was Monday of the Passion Week. I had come from the house of Lazarus where I had enjoyed a good breakfast prepared by Mary and served to me by Martha. I know it is written that, because I was hungry, I stopped at the fig tree, but when I found no  fruit I cursed the tree, and according to the gospel, it immediately withered (Matthew 21:19).

What actually happened was that when I came upon the fig tree, I was not hungry but merely curious because it was not time for fig trees to bare fruit. When I saw leaves on the tree, I thought I may also see fruit, which was not the case. My disappointment did not cause me to curse the tree. As a matter of fact, I never cursed anything or anyone in my life. The tree did not miraculously begin to wither, and it was not Matthew who wrote those words, but another many years later who was interested in showing the divinity of my messiahship by means of giving me supernatural powers rather than understanding my soul development.

Taught at the Temple

When I preached in Palestine to the crowds and to the Jewish leaders, I taught the fulfillment of the old prophecies. I had discussions with opponents of the liberal concept of the law, and some of them were Pharisees who argued with me not in the vicious or  venomous vein that one reads in the New Testament (Matthew 23:29), but in the atmosphere that so often prevails when the views held are important and precious to each. I never sought to provoke the high priests by adopting a hostile attitude toward them, but urged them to believe that God's love was now available as it had been promised to the Hebrew nation through the word of the old prophets.

Before my death I taught at the Temple at Jerusalem (John 7:14). I was very much aware of the evils found among the Hebrew priesthood, and I was also convinced through my studies of the prophets of old, and through the teachings I received directly from God, that the priesthood was not essential to a religion calling for a direct relationship between God and man. My intention was not to harm or destroy the prevailing system that had been built up through the centuries to perpetuate the priesthood as an integral part of the religion of the Hebrew people.

The Hebrew nation had been established as one consecrated by the Almighty with the priesthood as the intermediary between God and the people. These men were the leaders of the Hebrew nation and were designated to be a light to the Gentiles (Luke 2:32), and who would eventually lead the pagan peoples on the path of true belief and worship of the one eternal God.

This was my first opportunity to present my claims as the Messiah before the chief priests and rulers and most learned Hebrews in matters pertaining to religion. I made it known to them that my mission was to proclaim the glad tidings of the New Covenant between Jehovah and the people of Israel (Hebrews 8:13), and that the divine love was now present and could be obtained by all who might seek it through the earnest longing of their soul. I was the visible sign of its presence, for in my soul reposed this love that is the nature and essence of God.

To the Hebrew rulers, my claims appeared false, for it had been prophesied that no one would know whence the Messiah would come (John 7:27). Whereas, I was well-known as being Jesus of Nazareth, they also knew my father Joseph and that he, too, was born in Bethlehem.

In the census count it was deemed that the town where a man lived most of his life was the place he was associated with, not the one in which he was born. Thus, Jerusalem was considered the city of the great King David, rather than Bethlehem, where he was born. This type of argument showed recourse to technicalities by the priests in their determination not to recognize me as the Messiah. They felt that a redeemer of the people would upset their high position as the religious leaders of the nation, which they were unwilling to relinquish.

I replied to their minute scriptural objections on their own terms by proclaiming that it was not true that they knew where I was from or who my father was, because they referred to Joseph as my father whom they knew well, but I was referring to my Heavenly Father, whom they did not know (John 8:19).

Neither did they know whence I came, nor how or when I was created as a divine soul. The references of the rabbis to my father Joseph, were later eliminated from the gospels, for mention of my earthly parents was a thorn in the side of the later revisionists. They labored zealously to make me a god-man born of a virgin and the second person of a supposed trinity, which of course has no foundation in fact.

These technicalities were a subterfuge and the means of debating issues that were dear to the priest's hearts by laying emphasis on hair-splitting, intellectual distinctions. These resulted from subtle interpretations of the law, which were foreign to the real issues and the spiritual insight achieved through soul-seeking to know the truth.

When I quoted Isaiah, I stated that God told him, "Incline your ear and come unto me, hear and your soul shall live, and I will make an everlasting covenant with you, even as the sure mercies of David. Behold, I have given him as a witness to the people, a leader and commander to the people" (Isaiah 55:3-4). This was known to all who received religious instruction, and from it they knew that as a descendant of the House of David I had been appointed over them.

I told them that they should accept me as their Messiah, inasmuch as I had come from the lineage of their great King. I explained that I had come to enable their souls to live by showing them the way to the gift of immortality through God's divine love accompanied with the power of healing, which I performed to attest to the truth of my mission.

I further informed the priests that if they wished to determine the truth of my words, they should test my teachings that this love is now available and to pray in earnest for it. If they do with sincerity, this love will be conveyed to them and will change their soul's quality, by which sign they would know that it was present within.

I also stated that these teachings were not mine but those of my Heavenly Father, who had commanded me to proclaim them to the children of Israel, and, having been sent by him, I could do nothing of my own (John 8:28). What power I had, I received directly from God, and I never said that I could do what I saw the Father do, or imitate him as the gospel states (John 5:19), for that would give me power equal to that of God, which is blasphemy. This revision was added many years later for no mortal or spirit will ever through all of eternity have the power equal to that of God, the Almighty, Creator of the heavens and the earth.

Last Supper

The first holiday of the sacred year is Passover, which begins at sundown the 15th of Nissan (March-April) and continues for eight days. It celebrates the deliverance of the Hebrews from slavery in Egypt by Moses and requires the presence of every male over twelve years of age before the sanctuary of the Lord.

The Passover Festival is multifaceted: from brief spiritualism, with the invisible appearance of the prophet Elijah, to mystic messianism, and references to the Afikomen (the broken, hidden matzah), but this festival is essentially national and patriotic. Except for a certain break that took place several hundreds of years before my birth (presumably the Babylonian captivity),

Hebrews have gathered together to tell of this great march to freedom and the Lord protecting the Hebrews from Pharaoh's army, whose chariots and soldiers perished in the rising tide of the sea.

This safe exodus was so extraordinary in nature that Hebrews of all ages and times are commanded to feel as though this delivery had been done unto them personal-

ly. Annual instruction is given to the young, illustrated by history and embellished by tradition. This is the festival of liberty I loved and observed faithfully during my life, and it was during this festival that I chose to return to Jerusalem, where I met death in the performance of my mission as the Messiah of God.

When my disciples and I went to celebrate the Passover at Jerusalem, I remained near Bethany. I did not go up to the feast because I feared trouble with the Jewish authorities, so I switched my plans to go to Jerusalem at a time when I was least expected (John 7:10). Thus, I would be able to make my appearance and teach there without being stopped by the Jewish authorities or cause a disturbance between them and my disciples. I knew that once I was in the city, they would not dare to molest me.

My parents went on to Jerusalem to arrange for the preparation of the Upper Room. Since my coming was fraught with danger, it was decided that Peter and John would make known our readiness by meeting a young man with a pitcher near the Kedron stream, and he would take us to the room for the occasion (Mark 14:13). While it is not mentioned in the gospels, and many have conjectured as to the identity of this person with the pitcher, I should like to inform you that he was the writer of a gospel and his name was John Mark.

In the evening I joined my disciples and before we began the Passover meal, I said to Peter, "If I wash thee not, thou hast no part of me" (John 13:8), but Peter objected to this ablution. My purpose in this was to use the word "wash" not as a natural cleansing of the body nor even a symbol of the spiritual cleansing by baptism, but I meant the washing away of sin. I had to use symbolism in order to make my teachings concrete, and something that my disciples could understand.

I told them, "If ye love me, you will keep my commandment that ye love one another even as I have loved you" (John 15:12). This was the eleventh commandment and was above the Ten Commandments of Moses. It was the law of love, and obedience to this commandment would bring my disciples together. I wanted them not merely to love one another, but all mankind, for "one another" was a term that meant not only for a small circle, but for all people. This was the only commandment I gave to my disciples, and no other.

I never said in teaching my disciples the Lord's Prayer, that they should pray not to be led into temptation. I did say to be thankful for your daily bread.

Transubstantiation

I never said that my flesh or my blood should be consumed in order for my followers to attain salvation (John 6:54). The conception that the wine and bread were my blood and body was not a Hebrew one, but was very popular and was practiced among the Greeks. The cult of Dionysius, Orpheus, Isis and others sacrificed animals to the gods and ate their flesh and drank their blood under the impression or illusion that in this mystical rite the animal sacrificed represented the god. Thus by eating the animal's flesh and drinking its blood the devotee became at-one, at least temporarily, with the god himself.

These Greek ideas together with others found their way into the Christian ceremonies. The concept of the  transubstantiation of the blood and flesh came from pagan rites and was adopted for the deification of me as the Son of God. Thus, the combination of elements that comprise the eucharist was given the stamp of authenticity by the Greek writers of the second century.

I do not want to be remembered for the tragedy on the cross, which was the result of the malice and envy of the Jews, and the blood spilt is not an element that enters into God's plan of salvation. Besides, with this sacrament there is always more or less the worshipping of me as God, which is blasphemous and an act that I deplore. I do not want men to believe that they can be saved by any sacrifice on my part or by any blood that I may have shed as a result of my crucifixion.

As a matter of fact, I told my disciples, "The two greatest truths are: God is love and you must be born again" (John 3:3). Then you will find as you are transformed by divine love that you will, by your very nature, follow all the other Commandments. You will love your neighbor as yourself and, seeking first the kingdom of God, all else will be added unto you (Matthew 6:33). The New Covenant of the heart prophesied by Ezekiel and Jeremiah (Jeremiah 31:31) is the grace of God's love and is available to all who should seek to obtain it through prayer. I have shown the way to receive it, the living waters from the everlasting fountainhead of God's divine love.

Betrayal and Arrest

My mission was not imposed upon me, but shall I say I imposed it upon myself. This was because I had to be true to myself and faithful to my Heavenly Father, who had sent me to declare the glad tidings of the New Heart (Ezekiel 18:31). The day preceding my arrest I taught in the vicinity of the Temple, and it thundered, so that some of the people who were listening to my discourse thought that an angel, or God, had spoken from heaven. The weather was cold for, as it is recorded in the New  Testament, Peter had to warm his hands in the courtyard of the high priests (John 18:18). It was not in April that I was arrested and put to death, but it took place in March.

I understood that my mission had to continue regardless of the threats against my life. I knew there was danger and possible consequences, but I expected to be able to escape, and I would have, had it not been for the impulsiveness of my youngest and most impetuous disciple, Judas.

I never taught that my death on the cross was ordained by God or that Judas should betray me. In fact, my death was never a part of that which God considered necessary in the performance of my mission. Although, it was certain that I would die, the manner of my death was not foreordained as it is written (Matthew 20:19).

I never told any of my brothers or sisters, as it is recorded in the New Testament, that my time had not yet come while their time was opportune, always (John 7:6). That would mean that I had an understanding when I would be arrested and handed over to the Roman authorities for execution. I want to emphasize that I did not know when my time would come.

Judas was impatient with the peoples slowness to learn the truths that I had come to teach, so he went to the chief priests and told them he would help them capture me. The thirty pieces of silver they offered him was incidental, for his desire was for me to show them my power. Judas was so convinced of my sonship to God that he believed a legion of angels would descend in all their power and  glory to protect me from harm. I did not know beforehand that Judas would betray me, and I never said, "All of you are not clean" (John 13:11), referring to Judas, for I did not suspect him of any treachery and, as a matter of fact, when he betrayed me, I was taken by surprise.

Because I had been arrested, instead of overpowering the authorities, Judas regretted his impetuous actions. He took the thirty pieces of silver back to the chief priests (Matthew 27:3), saying, "I only wanted you to recognize the importance of my Master." They said to him that why he informed was of no concern to them, for now they had me where they wanted me. Judas threw the thirty pieces of silver at their feet and, feeling remorseful beyond endurance, went off and hanged himself. The priests took up the silver, as they looked upon it as blood money, did not want it in their treasury. After consultation they decided to buy a field of clay with it to bury strangers, known as Potter's Field (Matthew 27:3-7).

Judas was not a bad man as he has been depicted. His betrayal was not for silver or the purpose of gratifying any avarice or because of any jealousy or desire to revenge a wrong. Instead, it was because he was impulsive and had such belief in my powers and my ability to overcome the religious leaders in their fight to defeat the objects of my mission. He thought he would be doing me and the cause a great service by having it demonstrated to the authorities that I could not be silenced or harmed by any act of theirs. Judas' betrayal was really an act that grew out of his love for me and belief in the greatness of my powers. He was the youngest of my disciples and was not so easily controlled in his impulses and acts as

he would have been, had he been older.

At my arrest by the hirelings of the high priests in the Garden of Gethsemane, as it is mentioned in the New Testament, a youth who was present at the time of my betrayal was seized, and he had to tear himself away from the clutches of the hirelings. In the process he lost his outer garment of linen, which left him stripped, but he subsequently escaped (Mark 14:51). The apostle who originally wrote this statement was Mark, and the name of this youth was James, who was my younger brother, known as "the lesser." The reason the hirelings seized James was because he resembled me so much in face and figure that sometimes he was mistaken for me. Some of the hirelings thought that he was really I and that I was really he, and so they sought to arrest him to make certain that they had apprehended the right man.

My brother loved me very much and had begun to believe in my mission to the extent of his capabilities. He followed me when I was arrested, his heart breaking with anxiety and grief. The copyists of the original gospel eliminated the name of my brother and inserted the words "a certain youth" (Mark 14:51) because they did not want to use the word "brother", for it denoted what is really a fact, that my mother was the mother of seven children in the flesh besides myself. The writer also sought to enhance my prestige with readers of the New Testament by showing them to what degree I was able to inspire the devotion and loyalty of a stranger.

It is not true that in the garden Peter, or any one of my other followers, with a sword cut off the ear of Malchus (Matthew 26:51), a servant of the high priests. Peter did not wear a sword but merely a fishing knife. Furthermore, a hostile blow would have meant that the servants and hirelings of the high priests might have retaliated and clubbed our followers unmercifully as a consequence, a fact which Peter knew, as we all did at the time.

Jurisdiction

The Jewish court was not permitted by their Roman overlords to carry out their own sentence of my death, so after I was beaten, they sent me to the Roman Procurator

(Pilate) with the accusation that I was attempting to cause a revolt against Caesar by claiming myself to be king of the Jews.

Pilate arrested me, then he sent me to Herod Antipas (Luke 23:7), who happened to be in Jerusalem at the time to observe the festivities of the Passover. Some time before, Pilate had ordered a number of Galileans to be killed, and this caused enmity between Pilate and Herod, who claimed that Pilate had no authority to execute the men, since, as Galileans, they were under his (Herod's) jurisdiction. This coolness was patched up on the occasion of my arrest, for Pilate used this opportunity to send me to Herod to ascertain whether or not I was under his jurisdiction as a Galilean.

When Herod discovered, through inquiry, that I was born in Bethlehem in Judea and not in Galilee, he returned me to Pilate and was pleased that Pilate had extended him the courtesy of consulting him to establish under whose jurisdiction my condemnation and punishment was to be meted out. This is the explanation for the healing of the breach between Pilate and Herod (Luke 23:12) and the reason for the latter's appearance on the scene at the time of my arrest.

Trial

In those latter days men had appeared and claimed to be specially anointed by God with missions to perform. They were able to gather around them people whom they impressed with their character and the truth of their teachings. They were permitted for a short time to declare their doctrines and make their claims then suddenly were brought to death by the decree of those in authority. These men have long been forgotten and their doctrines have disappeared from memory, only in the instance of my death have I been remembered through the ages.

My trial by the body of men known as the Sanhedrin was in accordance with a rudimentary decree of the Sadducean law. The Sadducees were aggravated and incensed at the thought that any mortal could call himself the son of God; not in merely the sense that all human beings are the sons and daughters of God, but in that I stated that, "I  was in the Father and the Father was in me" (John 14:10). I did not mean that the Father and I were the same person. What I meant was that the Father's own love was in my soul, which made me a part of His divinity and at-one with him. This seemed to the Jews to be blasphemy because to them it put me on an equal basis with God. They felt that such blasphemy could destroy the true meaning of Jehovah to the Hebrew people and I deserved death for it.

I was accused of breaking the Mosaic law when I healed on the Sabbath (Matthew 12:10). I had helped a mule out of a hole on that day, however, I did not break the law, for restoring the body is far more important than the Sabbath. To the consternation of those who set their store by rigid rules, I contended that the Sabbath was made for man and not man for the Sabbath (Mark 2:27). This meant that by putting life first as God intended, I was not going outside Hebrew law or even bringing a new God-given revelation to man, but was following and agreeing with the insight of Haggai, Hebrew prophet par excellence.

The Sadducees had a deep religious conviction and a sense of obligation to protect and keep whole the teachings of their faith. I stood in the position to them and their religion as a breeder of sedition; they saw me as an enemy and would-be destroyer of the doctrines of the Israelite nation and a seducer of the people. They considered me importunate to the Hebrew religion and a source of potential danger to their harmony with the Roman authorities.

It was the spring of the year 29 A.D., and I was thirty-six years old. My judges were willing to accept unfair means through perjured witnesses (Matthew 26:59) in order to eliminate me. They found me guilty of blasphemy and iconoclastic teachings against the beliefs of the Hebrew faith. I appeared not only guilty of treason to their national life, but also to the higher God-given life of their religious government.

My father, Joseph, was present at my unfair trial and watched me buffeted and condemned. There is evidence in the New Testament to show that, nine months before the crucifixion he was alive when I was preaching in Capernaum. The Jews asked each other, "Is not he the son of Joseph and Mary whom we know?" (John 6:42). This shows that they referred to my father as still living at the time.

My father was sick over the treatment I received and at the confirmation of his worst fears. His eyes were opened to the stagnant state of the Sanhedrin at the time, and he realized that what they considered religion was merely farce. He also realized the enormous gulf between their religion as practiced by its most august body and what I proposed in its place—not only to restore Judaism to its pristine purity and authority, but also to impart its culminating sublimity and grandeur.

The shame and humiliation that my father suffered at seeing his firstborn son condemned and executed as a criminal, bore in him the conviction of his son's innocence and the righteousness of his cause and the truth of his mission.

I went to my death, not so I could be a willing sacrifice in a bloody ritual condemned by a wrathful and exacting God, but because I was faithful to my Heavenly Father and refused to recant or deny my mission. In truth I was the Christ, possessor of God's divine love and nature, and I had been sent to teach the way to this love and to show the blessings that it brings.

The great element of tragedy in all this was that the Jews were so mistaken and failed to recognize and accept me as their long looked for Messiah and Redeemer, not from their material condition of bondage, but from the bondage of sin and error in which they had lived for so long.

The act of the Jews to cause my death has been called the "great crime of the world" and has caused the people themselves to be hated and destroyed as a nation. If my people had received me and accepted and followed my teachings, they would not have become the scattered and persecuted race that they have been for all these centuries.

Crucifixion

After my trial I was beaten by Roman soldiers and taken for crucifixion. I was accompanied on my weary march to the cross by a great host of spirits in whom was vested wonderful pow-ers all trying to sustain me. At the scene of the crucifixion it grew dark and cloudy (Mark 15:33), and there were those who thought that the darkness was an indication of God's anger at the deed. The fact is that God is love, and His love was open even to those who were responsible for my death. God did not express anger because He has none, and the storm that darkened that day over Jerusalem simply obeyed the natural order of an unsettled spring day for that time of the year.

There was no great concourse of people because many of my followers stayed away, fearing arrest. There were soldiers and a large number of the members of the Sanhedrin and a few of my followers were present to witness my execution. While on the cross, there was no sudden breaking up of nature or of material things, I did no talking because of the pain and exhaustion of my battered body.

Nevertheless, any words that I could have uttered could not have been heard by my followers who were present because they were kept away from the immediate scene of the execution. The nails that pierced my flesh were hammered into my wrists and not the palms, as has been widely believed. Physical death came to me through asphyxiation due to the unnatural position of my body hanging from my outstretched arms on the cross. The rite for the dying was administered to me and, after I had been pronounced dead, my followers were permitted to approach my body and remove it from the cross.

I died without fear, for in my soul was a knowledge that I could die only in the flesh and that I would retain my consciousness and identity after death. Not once did I lose faith in my Heavenly Father or in the truth of my mission. I never voiced any complaints or doubts that God was with me, nor did I call for help to cause the bitter cup to pass from me (Matthew 26:39), but I did ask whether I had done all that I could in the short time of my ministry.

I never spoke the words that I am supposed to have uttered while on the cross, "My God, my God, why have you forsaken me" (Matthew 27:46)? This is the opening line of the twenty-second Psalm, which was indeed messianic in nature, for it deals with the suffering of the afflicted. I did not say these words in order to fulfill the prophecy embodied in that Psalm, nor did I say what are supposed to be my last words on earth, "Into thy hands I commend my spirit" (Luke 23:46), in order to fulfill the saying of the old Scriptures (Psalms 31:5).

The truth of the matter is that after my death, the copyists searched and found these passages within the Psalms and, therefore, decided that I must have said them. Thus, when they wrote the account of my crucifixion, they added these sayings in order to show that I had done or said those things, which would fulfill Scripture.

It is true that there were two others who were crucified with me. They were also considered violators of the law and were to be punished by hanging on the cross. I was between them, but they did not speak to me, neither did one mock me nor did the other seek to be converted or ask me to pardon him. I did not say to him that he would be in paradise with me (Luke 23:43), for that was a boon that I could not grant. I had no authority to forgive sin, as it is wrongfully stated in various passages of the New Testament (Luke 5:24), for their places in the world of spirits would not depend upon me, but upon the condition of their souls as the result of their deeds while on earth.

The Roman centurion who officiated at the crucifixion was convinced of my innocence, but he never said  that I was the Son of God (Mark 15:39) because he did not understand that concept. Though he believed in my innocence and, at the Pentecost with the preaching of my disciples and his being convinced that I was resurrected, he converted to Christianity, as did others of the Roman soldiery.

You can forget the description found in the New Testament, which Matthew did not write at all, that deals with the opening of the graves and the letting loose of the spirits supposedly contained therein who ran about in the streets of Jerusalem showing themselves to many (Matthew 27:52-53). This is strictly out of the imagination of the gospel compilers and was written many years later, and is nothing more than a passage that the imaginative writers put into this work.

Why people should want to believe in the representations of things that never happened is hard for me to understand. In themselves they have no real significance except as an endeavor to make as dramatic and impressive as possible the supernatural circumstances they allege surrounded my death.

So you see, I am not a saviour because of my preferring the cross to denying being the Messiah, but I was simply performing my mission, and I would not be the Christ if I had not persisted to the end.

Atonement

I know that the belief in my sacrifice on the cross is the cornerstone of most of the churches, as stated in the New Testament and interpreted by the churches and the commentators of the gospels. They interpret that my death carries with it a meaning of some price I paid for the redemption of mankind from their sins (Matthew 20:28), and from the punishment that they would have to undergo for having committed these sins.

It is said in various parts of the New Testament that my blood washes away all sin (Revelation 1:5), and that my death on the cross satisfies God's demands for justice; there are many similar expressions conveying the same idea. However, these sayings of the Bible were not written by the persons to whom they are ascribed, but by writers who, in their various translations and reproductions added to and eliminated from the original writings, until the Bible became filled with false doctrines and teachings.

Christianity teaches that God sent his son, Jesus, to die on the cross to pay for the sins of the world. This assumes that the events leading up to my death and the men responsible were also necessary for this debt to be paid. If that were true, then why is it that Judas who betrayed me, Pilate who sentenced me, and the Jews who clamored for my death, are not considered to be saviours too, even if it might be in a secondary sense only, instead of their being thought of as traitors and villains?

Nowhere in the Old Testament writings does one find as an essential to God's promise of the Messiah that I had to die asphyxiated on a cross so that my Father in heaven, who had just revealed himself through me as a God of love, could satisfy a supposed wrath for the sins of man.

Some early Christian cults, mistaken in their understanding of the old Hebrew offerings, had made the loving Father into the executioner of his own son, a ritual that had been strikingly condemned by God in the case of Abraham. In accord with this mistaken notion of the Hebrew offerings—a conception never advanced by me or the apostles themselves, but by later pagan converts to Christianity—my blood, in a similar manner, as the pagan mystery cults believed, is supposed, in some mysterious way, to cleanse man's soul of evil thoughts, deeds and desires, doing vicariously what man himself does not make the effort to do, and this is supposed to make his soul fit to live in God's heaven.

Their mistake, however, lies in the erroneous belief of the Hebrews who thought that there was efficacy in the shed blood of sacrificed animals. They said "Life is in the blood" (Leviticus 17:11); a scientific view devoid of any religious implications. The Hebrew system, as demonstrated by the great prophets who brought the unchanging word of God to the people, uncompromisingly stressed forgiveness of sin through the turning to Jehovah their God and forsaking evil thoughts and deeds. Only in this way could the sins of man be forgiven.

The offerings of animals at the Temple in Jerusalem was simply an outward act of the priests to show that man's heart had turned to God and that he was walking in the statutes of the Torah. With the Babylonian captivity the Hebrews learned that man could walk in God's ways without a Temple or sacrifices, and that man's real offering to God, as expressed by Micah the prophet, consisted in obeying God's laws of love, justice and mercy (Micah 6:8).

Later, priestly insistence upon these rites and ceremonies was, for national purposes, to keep the Hebrews pure and apart from the Gentiles and later the pagan converts to Christianity. These converts were wedded to their own ritualistic cults.  They adopted and blended the rites of the Hebrews with their own and converted the religion that I brought to become a religion of rite and ritual, with salvation to be had through blood and sacrifice, with me as the victim.

In reading the passages in Luke and in Mark pertaining to the inheriting of eternal life (Luke 18:18), there is absolutely no reference to the vicarious atonement through my blood on the cross as the means of salvation.

When the rich young man came to me and asked me how he could gain salvation for his soul (Matthew 19:16), the way the New Testament describes this meeting between us leads the reader to assume that my great message to mankind was nothing more than the Ten Commandments of Moses. When the young man declared to me that he had obeyed all of the Commandments and that he wished to know what else he had to do for eternal life, I told him to give away all his property, become poor and to follow me (Matthew 19:21).

Well, this makes a nice story in the New Testament, and is one usually read with interest and accepted by all those who understand that the Ten Commandments given to the children of Israel were in reality the laws of

Jehovah pertaining to the moral code. However, they do not realize if that were all that I had come to teach, then there would be no need of Jesus, for Moses had already given these Commandments, and I could do nothing more than to confirm what Moses had already proclaimed. It is a fact that I did teach the laws of Moses because they do lead to purity, but not to the angelic state, which cannot be reached only by obedience to the moral code.

The conception of the vicarious atonement was a much later concept and never formed any part of the original writings of my disciples. This afterthought took form and shape when the teachings of the New Heart had been eliminated from the text in favor of the conception of salvation to conciliate the old Hebrew idea of sacrifice. They viewed me as being the sacrifice that would cleanse the sins of the world through the shedding of my blood.

This conception of the atonement is all wrong, for these writers were attempting to substitute me in place of the animals of sacrifice in the Hebrew plan of salvation. This is not justified by any teachings of mine nor by any of the true teachings of my disciples to whom I had explained the plan of salvation and what the atonement meant.

The consequence of this error is that the churches teach a salvation based on my sacrifice and death on the cross. I deplore this, for no sacrifice made by me or anyone else can atone for the sins and misdeeds of another, not even if it be by the Messiah. God is the Creator of life and of death, and my life already was a possession of God and, when I surrendered it, I did not give to God anything that was not already his. The absurdity of believing that God demanded that I should die in order to make a satisfactory payment is so apparently false that

I and all the spirits living in God's kingdom wonder how mortals can believe such an unreasonable dogma.

The idea of a salvation based on the shedding of my blood has done much harm to retard the spiritual growth of believers in this doctrine while they live on earth and when they go to the spirit world. I want the world to know that my mission was not to bring redemption through my suffering and death, but to bring immortal life through God's love and mercy.

Despite this great error, there are enough truths in the Bible that have survived to lead men to salvation, especially those that show the way to attain moral perfection, which was one of the objects of my teachings when on earth, but not the great object of my mission.

THE REAPPEARANCE

Burial

My father, Joseph, came to Jerusalem with me on my last fatal mission that ended in my crucifixion. It was he who received permission from the authorities to take my body for burial after the Roman lancer, Coriginus, poked his lance into my side to determine my death (John 19:34).

When death came to me, my soul arose from the cross encased in its spirit body. I accompanied my body as it was carried by my followers to a place not far from the site of execution that my father had purchased for my burial.

Nicodemus arrived with a mixture of myrrh and aloes and they cleansed my body and wound it in linen cloth with spices in the manner that was the custom of the day  (John 19:39-40). I observed the events, waiting until the ritual of burial had been completed, then I ascended to the spirit world from the Mount of Olives. My entrance into the spirit world was a glorious one. I was welcomed by many spirits and by the Father. I proclaimed to the inhabitants the re-bestowal of the availability of divine love and the possibility of the at-onement with God that it brings.

The next day the chief priests went to Pilate and appealed to him that the sepulcher be made secure until the third day so that I would not arise as promised. Pilate agreed and sent guards to seal the tomb and set a watch (Matthew 27:65-66). My father was very interested in the precautions taken to prove that I would not arise from the tomb, so he kept watch along with the soldiers. Because he feared the Jews as well as the Romans, he sought to conceal his identity by taking the name Joseph of Arimathea.

On the third day I left the spirit realms and returned to the earth plane and entered the tomb. I dematerialized my battered body of flesh and blood into the surrounding atmosphere. I was able to do this because I understood and had the power to call into operation certain laws of nature. I then materialized a new body with the elements drawn from the universe, which to a degree was like flesh and blood closely resembling my own body.

I created this new body for my return by the culling of the spiritual matter of the universe to give my spirit body an appearance and density similar to flesh. This process conforms to the spiritual laws that causes organic molecules to build up the density of a spirit body. This rebuilding, or materialization, took place in a way similar in the way that ectoplasm is borrowed from a medium and used to enable a spirit body to become visible to mortal sight. This process of transformation from spiritual matter to physical matter, like unto flesh, without the benefit of a bodily organism took place by my own spiritual energy being applied to the spiritual matter of the universe.

I took up the linen cloth which had wrapped my body and folded it neatly and placed it in a corner of the tomb (John 20:6). At the time, I did not realize that this fabric would be the means of a fairly good representation of the appearance of my countenance. I left the tomb by passing through the rock that barred the entrance. Later on, the stones blocking the entrance to the cave were rolled away by the bright spirit in the form of a young man who was sent by God for this purpose (Matthew

28:2). The strength he displayed in this task was obtained through the transmission of energy conveyed to him by many spirits who were present at the time. He used a guard whom he put into trance by suggestion as the means to obtain the necessary ectoplasm to bring about his materialization.

When the guards realized my body had disappeared, they relayed what they had seen to the chief priests who, after consultation, decided they would bribe the guards to say to the people that my body had been stolen from the tomb by my disciples. The guards were promised to be kept in good standing with Pilate if he should hear of the deception (Matthew 28:12-14). My father was there when the angel came and rolled the stones away. He was frightened and overcome when he saw the shining one standing guard at the tomb entrance. Later he heard Mary Magdalene inquiring as to the whereabouts of her beloved Master (John 20:2).

When I revealed myself to Mary, she did not recognize me, for my appearance was not the same as that of the Jesus whose body had been entombed. Although I did have the same countenance and voice of affection that were familiar to her, my physical appearance was

different and she thought that I was the gardener (John 20:15). Peter arrived and was astonished. He did not comprehend the events and was bewildered (Luke 24:12) as were the others, notwithstanding what I had told them prior to my crucifixion (Mark 9:31).

No one at the time understood the power I had over matter. People have taught and believed that my body arose from the tomb and that the bodies of mortals will also arise at the time of the great resurrection. This is not the case because the body that dies disintegrates into its elements, and never again will these elements form that same body. There are laws set forth familiar to mortals from their observations of the workings of nature, that prove the impossibility of such an occurrence.

After my death my father was confused as to what my mission was, and he was bewildered by the turn of events and feared for his safety. He was also terribly disappointed at my being king of the Jews only in the sign of the cross in which they inscribed me as such in several languages (Luke 23:38).

Resurrection

Prior to my death I never said there would be a resurrection of my physical body, for the body that is once laid in the grave will never be resurrected. What I did say

to my followers was that I would not die because my soul was immortal and therefore not subject to death. However, I had great difficulty being understood by the people because of their lack of spirituality at the time and their inability to perceive that I was not talking of physical death but of spiritual death.

The body of flesh is matter. Like all matter it is used only for life on the earth and can never be used for any function or for the clothing of any spirit in the spirit world. I know it has been written that certain prophets of old were translated to the spirit heavens clothed in their fleshly bodies (2 Kings 2:11), but it is impossible for such a thing to be so. The same laws apply to the physical body of a saint as that of a sinner; flesh and blood cannot inherit the kingdom of heaven, and no belief or teaching can make true what is not.

When I said "He that liveth and believeth on me shall never die" (John 11:26), what I meant was that the man whose soul was not dead in sin but believed in the teachings that I declared, would experience God's forgiveness and mercy, and that that man will live forever in God's kingdom.

My teachings were that the mortal at death would arise in a spirit body (1 Corinthians 15:44). This is not a new body made especially for this occasion, but one that had been with that person throughout his earthly life. The spirit body is necessary to a soul's existence and is that part that manifests the senses of the soul.

The resurrection that I taught is not the resurrection of the physical body, but of the spirit body, and not from death, for it never dies, rather from its envelopment in the flesh. Thus, you can realize that the resurrection will not take place at some unknown day in the distant future but will take place at the very moment the physical body dies. This resurrection applies to all mortals, for all who have ever lived and died have been resurrected, and all hereafter who shall live and die will also be resurrected. So, you see, the belief that the spirits of men who have died the natural death are resting in their graves or in some state of oblivion, in order to come again to life and be resurrected, is not true.

When I said, "I am the way, the truth, and the life," (John 14:6) I did not mean, "Wait until I die and then I will demonstrate the resurrection, or when you see me ascend to heaven, then I will become the resurrection and you will know it". The meaning of this saying and that of my mission was to show the way how to become a partaker of God's gift of divine love.

This love was made available to the first man and woman, who were created just a little lower than angels. They were given the privilege of becoming divine angels and acquiring immortal souls. Instead they chose to be independent of God and thought they could become immortal through their own efforts. The parts played by the apple and the snake and the devil, of course, are not literally true, but are merely symbolic of the elements that entered into their temptation and fall.

With the first man and woman's disobedience, or refusal to seek God's love in the prescribed manner, they lost the potential of receiving it for themselves and their descendants. With this loss man was limited to making his way in the physical world through those finite human qualities, namely the will, the intellect and the moral fiber. In fact, before the rebestowal with my coming no one could obtain the condition that this potential made possible by any aspirations or efforts on his part, no matter how great the effort might be, for the divine qualities were simply not available. The rebestowal of the potential was not in itself the actual bestowal of the divine love, but merely made it possible for the divine qualities to be acquired through aspiration and effort.

The possibility of this love had not been restored to man in all the long centuries, and men had remained in this condition of death until it was brought to light by me. So you see, the resurrection from death that I taught arises from the fact that God had withdrawn the potential for man to receive His divine love and that, with my coming, the privilege had been restored.

Now in order to obtain this resurrection, one must seek this love and thereby become a child of God's resurrection. This resurrection was not possible for any prophet, seer, reformer or teacher of any faith before my coming, no matter how excellent their moral teachings and personal lives might have been.

When I received God's precious gift of divine love, I came into possession of God's divine nature, and it was then that I realized my at-onement with my Father and I had a consciousness of my immortality, and I knew that I had been lifted up unto everlasting life.

Road to Emmaus

It became impossible for my father to remain in Palestine, having been pointed out as the father of the crucified Jesus. He was afraid of the consequences, both political as well as religious, of my crucifixion. So, that afternoon under the concealed name of Cleopas, my father and my brother Thomas, hastened to Emmaus (Luke 24:13) to escape what they thought was going to be certain arrest and crucifixion as had happened to me. I went after them in order to bring them back to Jerusalem

so that all my disciples would be together when I spoke to them.

Thomas had begun to doubt, and his attitude could have been disastrous to the entire plan of salvation by bringing pessimism and skepticism into the minds of my other disciples. That is why I went to Emmaus and had

Thomas and Cleopas recognize me when I broke bread with them (Luke 24:30-31). Seeing me in my recreated body immediately caused them to regain their faith and the next morning they returned with me to Jerusalem to face whatever dangers might await. It didn't take long for Thomas to loose his faith, and on the next Friday when he poked his fingers into my side (John 20:27), what he expe-

rienced amazed him and it restored his faith in me as the resurrected Christ, and this crucial time was overcome in victory.

In Jerusalem where all my disciples were assembled, I told them that all the power of heaven and earth comes to those who partake of God's love (Matthew 28:18). I said to them, "Go, therefore, and teach the way to receive this love for every man can be baptized by the holy spirit through his desire (Mark 1:8), and by this God's love will develop in your soul and it will be with you all the days of your life, forever with me and at-one with God."

My return in a recreated body was necessary in order to show my disciples that I was still alive even after death by crucifixion. For at this time in their spiritual development this phenomenon was proof in their eyes that I was the Messiah of God. Their real understanding of my messiahship came to them at the Pentecost when the divine love was conveyed into their souls with such power and abundance that they knew I had come to bring the way to the very essence and nature of God.

My death was a great personal tragedy in the lives of my nearest and dearest. My mother stayed with John and his family until her death (John 19:27). John's love and affection for her were a great source of consolation. In the loss of my life I also lost the physical ties to my family. But now in the spirit life where every member of my family is present and often with me, they have gained a full realization of my mission and of my love for them.

Pentecost

My followers who had remained faithful to me after my crucifixion had the realization that my mission was a spiritual one. They were very much affected by the brutal manner in which my death had been imposed upon me. Their sorrow was deep and continual, and it was their love for me and their grieving that turned their hearts toward God in a great yearning for solace. They loved me wholeheartedly as their rabbi and were filled with deep grief that made their souls ready to receive the divine love when it was poured out upon them.

The love culminated in great abundance when it was conveyed to them fifty days after my death at the time of the pentecostal showering upon their souls of God's precious essence. It came to their souls with a great inflowing and burning of the heart and with the sound of a mighty rushing wind that shook the room where they were assembled and filled them with its power (Acts 2:2). This meant that it came into their souls in such abundance that they were shaken to the extent that they thought the house in which they were assembled was disturbed. In this, they were mistaken, for the presence of the holy spirit does not affect things of inanimate nature, but is confined to and is exclusively for the human soul. The love in their souls did not come all at once,

77

but had been building up within them for those fifty days since my death.

After the Pentecost my disciples had gained a clearer understanding of my mission. The inflowing of God's love absorbed their human or natural love and gave them the faith and courage that they needed to set out into the world and preach the doctrines of my mission—the love of God for His children and the fact that this love was waiting for any and all who should seek it.

The Pentecost marked the end of the Jewish dispensation or the end of the Jewish world in that the Mosaic laws, the highest available prior to my coming, were now superseded by the New Covenant of the heart (Hebrews 8:8) and the rebirth of the soul. At this time the divine love that was first bestowed upon me was now being granted to my followers in great abundance.

Holy Spirit

The churches of today believe and teach that the holy ghost is the third part of a trinity having various names connected with it, such as the spirit of God, spirit of the Lord, spirit of Christ, spirit of truth, spirit of glory, the paraclete, the advocate, the comforter and the strengthener.

The holy spirit is as invisible as the wind, yet it is just as real and existing. It is an energy of God that manifests His love, care and presence. This spirit does not communicate with mortals or spirits directly, nor does it appeal to their reasoning faculties. It cannot instruct or inform, but operates upon the human mind indirectly to influence a man's reasoning. I have never been instructed by the holy spirit, whose function is not that of teaching, but of conveying God's divine qualities to the human soul.

Now the spirit of God is not the holy spirit, though it is a part of God. This spirit demonstrates to men the operation of God in other directions and for other purposes. It has to do with the governing of the matter of the universe. This is God's creative spirit, caring spirit and the spirit that makes effective the laws and designs for the governing of the universe. It has been manifest throughout eternity and is the spirit that has been described in Genesis, hovering over the face of the waters (Genesis 1:2). This spirit has worked on the earth developing it in preparation for the day when living beings would inhabit it.

All things have their existence, operation and growth in the spirit of God as evidenced in many varied ways in human experience. Hence, when men say that they live and move and have their being in God, what they should mean is that they live, move and have their being in God's spirit. It is the source of life and light and health and numerous other blessings that humans possess and enjoy. The energy of this spirit is omnipresent and universal in its existence and workings.

Now the holy spirit is as distinctive from the spirit of God as the human soul is distinctive from all other creations. The holy spirit is that part of God that has to do exclusively with the relationship between God and man. The subject of its operation is divine love, and the object of its workings is the human soul. The great goal to be reached by its operation is the transformation of the human soul from the image of God, as it was created, into the very essence and substance of God, with immortality as the result.

This gift is so high and sacred and merciful that the part of God that carries the divine love to man and accomplishes the great miracle of rebirth is called the "holy spirit".

Trinity

I know that Christians generally believe and classify the holy spirit as being a part of the Godhead, identical and equal to God, though having a different and distinct personality. The orthodox preachers and theological writers teach that it is a fact that the Father, Son and Holy Ghost are one, coequal and coexisting, and this fact is the great mystery of God. Men have been taught that they should not try to fathom this mystery because these sacred things are God's alone, and it is unlawful for men to enter into these secrets.

This declaration and admonition are very wise as the wisdom of men goes and spares the expounders of this doctrine of mystery from having to explain what they cannot, because it is impossible for them to unravel what, as a fact, has no reality. All through the ages men have sought to understand this "great mystery", as they call it, and have been unsuccessful.

The early Church fathers met with the same defeat in  their endeavors to understand this mystery and then, because of their defeat, declared the explanation of this doctrine to be a secret of God and not to be inquired into by man, for it belonged to God alone. Thus, from the beginning of the established church after my death and the death of my apostles, it was declared that the doctrine of the trinity, one in three and three in one, was the vital foundation stone of their visible Church's existence.

Now, from time to time there arose men who had more enlightenment than their brothers within the

Church, and they attempted to gainsay the truth of this doctrine and declared and maintained that there was only one God, the God of Abraham. But they were in the minority and, because these men did not act with the more powerful, their views were rejected. Thus, this great mystery became the Church's sacred symbol of power and truth, unexplainable and therefore more certain and entitled to even more credence.

It seems to be the tendency of men, or at least of those who believe in the Bible as the inspired word of God, to welcome and encourage as the more wonderful and important and the more to be cherished, those things that savor of the mysterious, rather than those things that may be learned and understood.

It is true that I discussed Abraham with the Jews and how he would have welcomed my appearance in Jerusalem, but I never saw Abraham until I went to the spirit world, regardless of what the gospels declare I said. Nor did I say that I existed before Abraham (John 8:58), which would falsely make me the second part of a trinity and a part of the Godhead. This is an insertion that was put into John's gospel a hundred years or more after John had written his original work.

I never claimed to be part of the Godhead, for nowhere in the Bible is there any saying of mine that God is tripartite consisting of the Father, Son and Holy Ghost. As a matter of fact, never when I was on earth did I teach such a doctrine, but only this: that God is the Father the only God, and that I, Jesus, am his Son the "first fruits" of the resurrection (1 Corinthians 15:23), and that the Holy Ghost is God's messenger for conveying the divine love and, as such, brings the comforter (John 14:26).

Evangelization

When I sent my disciples forth in pairs to teach (Mark 6:7), I did not enable them to heal the sick or cure the blind, the lame and the crippled because it was not in my power to do so. Such power could only be obtained from God as a result of the divine love being in their souls to the extent that they would be possessed of the power to heal (Luke 9:1). This power could then be used in obedience to the prayers for healing on the part of my disciples. So the New Testament is wrong in that particular, for they could not heal until the day of the Pentecost, when the divine love flowed into their souls in such abundance that they were given this power.

After seeing my newly materialized body at the tomb, my father experienced a great transformation in his beliefs about my mission and began to see it in its true spiritual sense for the first time. When his confusion and bitter disappointment subsided, he gained faith in my mission as the Messiah, and to calm his anguished heart he evangelized with some of my disciples on several of the islands off the coast of Greece, notably Patmos and Cyprus. After many years he made his way to Britain, but died there soon after. The supernatural event connected with the flowering of a branch has no factual relation to the events that mark his stay on that island empire.

My brothers Thomas and Judah became my apostles, and my brother Jacob founded the Jerusalem sect. These followers and others had managed to plant in the souls of the succeeding generation of people the seeds for prayer to God that saves the soul and gives immortal life.

Peter

There is nothing in the gospels that indicates Peter had received primacy for, as a matter of fact, he was not the first to recognize that I was the Messiah; the first to do so was my cousin John. When the gospels were written, the Christian movement was under way and the account that stressed that Peter had acknowledged me to be the Christ (Matthew 16:16), does not show that I had ever bestowed leadership upon him. Any statements that indicate that Peter discovered my identity through heavenly grace are not true (Matthew 16:17). This was simply inserted to strengthen and give authority to the Church's claim that I had bestowed primacy upon him as my successor.

I never gave Peter the keys to the kingdom, for the only key is the divine love, which can be possessed by all  mortals and spirits who desire to open its gate. Nor did I give Peter the power to bind and loosen in heaven those things that he might find appropriate for him to do on earth (Matthew 16:19), for this was something that I never said and never gave. It came from a later Greek writer and was written into the gospel of Matthew as legal authority. I could not make Peter a representative of God on earth nor ratify those acts that he felt should be done. Only God could designate a mortal to be his representative, as had been done in the case of the Hebrew prophets and John the Baptist, and, in a different way, myself.

Now with respect to the saying, "Upon this rock I shall build my church" (Matthew 16:18), this is a distortion of what I said to Peter committed by the later gospel writers. When I said, "Thou art Peter," I did not say, "Upon this rock I shall build my church," meaning neither upon Peter nor myself, but upon the Rock of Ages—the Father, through the divine love that had been brought to light with my coming.

Peter's leadership was recognized because he was the eldest, held the respect of the other disciples and was looked up to because of his close relationship with me. Oftentimes I had addressed him while I was teaching my disciples and had favored him by taking him with me to the Mount of Transfiguration. Peter spoke boldly at the Pentecost, and he preached and healed on the Mediterranean coast and in various parts of the Greek world. He never recalled from the dead the person of Tabitha in Joppa, as recorded in the New Testament (Acts 9:40), but healed her of her illness. No one can recall to life a person who has died.

Peter continued my work and gained in love and his conviction of the truths that I taught him. His pre-eminence was the result of the practical turn of events, for he took the leadership upon himself, which was enhanced when he sent Barnabas to Asia Minor on various missions. Peter worked consistently to establish the church and eliminate undesirable traits to make it a firm religious institution. He decided that many innovations had to be adopted if the pagans were to become believers in me and my message.

Peter made his way to Rome, where he was arrested and then released from prison. This was not by any miracle of an angel coming to take the irons from his wrists and opening the door (Acts 12:7), but because some of his jailers had become believers in me and my teachings and were converted. They had seen Peter heal and preferred the things of the spirit rather than to see him languish in prison and perhaps suffer the same fate as I.

After my death questions concerning the movement were referred to Peter for solution. He showed himself capable of holding the leadership and also because Rome being the leader of the known world at the time and, as Peter was the authority of the greatest church in the greatest city of the world, he became the authority over the entire Christian world. He lived in Rome for nearly fifteen years and was crucified there about the same time as was Paul, shortly before the destruction of the Temple in 70 A.D.

Paul

Paul was a very learned man among the Jews and was a strict believer and follower of the Pharisees' doctrines. He knew nothing about divine love, for he had never experienced it, nor did he understand what it was intellectually.

My summons to Paul was not only for the purpose of stopping his persecution of my people (Acts 9:4), but also  to enlist him in my service. I realized that my doctrines must be preached not only among the learned Jews, but also among the Gentile philosophers. Since my followers were not educated or learned men, I saw that I must have a disciple who would have the mental qualifications to present my teachings to these men in a convincing way, and to be able to withstand their logic and reasoning.

When I summoned Paul on his way to Damascus, he was felled to the ground by the brightness of the great light that shone about him (Acts 9:3). Paul heard what I said and answered me and went into the town, but he was not blind, nor did the prophet Ananias do anything to him in the way of curing any physical blindness (Acts 9:17). Ananias only helped to open the spiritual blindness of Paul and showed him the way to the love of man and the love of God.

Paul did not have the love that John did. Whenever John would come in close communion with the common people, he could, by the great power and influence of his love, persuade them to embrace and receive my teachings and, as a consequence, feel the inflowing of the divine love. Paul did not have this love to such an extent, hence, I intended his mission to be more of teaching my truths to the intellect and mental perceptions of the people of greater intellectual development than those with whom John and the other disciples would come in contact.

Paul eventually acquired divine love to a considerable degree, but in his early ministry he had doubt at times of my call to him to do this work. His doubt was his besetting sin or thorn in the flesh from which he suffered (2 Corinthians 12:7). Nevertheless, he became a wonderful power to spread my truths and to convince men that the love of God was the great possession to be obtained.

Paul caused his hearers to believe in me as the son of God and the messenger to declare to the world the great plan of man's salvation. When he said, "They see through a glass darkly, but then they shall see face to face" (1

Corinthians 13:12), he meant that the people will see such evidence and manifestations that they will know that they and their brethren are all sons of the one living God.

Paul never taught that I was God, nor did he believe that I was, and whenever it is set forth that he said that, or rather what is written on this subject and interpreted to mean that I am God (Philippians 2:6), that interpretation is erroneous.

You may also rest assured that the book of Hebrews was not written by Paul, who had already entered the spirit world many years before this epistle had been written. Instead, this book was written by a Greek supporter of the Hellenistic turn that Christianity had taken after Titus's destruction of Jerusalem.

Authenticity of the Bible

The churches differ in their creeds and government and interpretations of the Bible, yet they, the orthodox churches, are all founded upon the Bible. They cannot teach greater or other truths than what the Bible contains. Hence, if one is seeking truths that are not  contained in the Bible, one's inquiries cannot be answered by those whose knowledge is confined strictly to the teachings of the Bible.

As now written, the Bible is a grand old book and does preserve a number of my saying and teachings. However, it is not the true mouthpiece of God in many particulars and is a stumbling block to man acquiring a correct knowledge of the truths of God. I tell you that God's truths are simple and can be understood by all men without the need of a highly developed intellect. Any religion that cannot be understood by the ordinary exercise of the mental faculties cannot be a true religion.

My disciples and followers did not commence to place my teachings or the experiences of my life in manuscript form until long after I had left the earth. They expected my speedy return, at which time I would become their king and legislator. Hence, they saw no reason or necessity to preserve in written form the truths that I had instructed them in.

The Bible was compiled from many writings, and the compilers in those early times differed in their opinions, just as men do now regarding religion. The more powerful of these men had the authority to declare what should be accepted according to their interpretations of the manuscripts that were being copied. These men put forth the copies to be made in accordance with their ideas and, I may say, desires to attain power and control over the common people in their beliefs and observances of religious worship. They, in turn, put forth such productions to be true copies of the original manuscripts.

As these copies were successively made, the preceding ones were destroyed. Thus, the earliest existing writings of the gospels came from copies that came into existence many years after the original manuscripts from which they are claimed to have been compiled were written.

These men over time had become less spiritual than my disciples, and their thoughts and efforts became more centered in building up the Church than in attempting to develop and preserve my great spiritual teachings. The God of love then, to a great extent, became the God of hatred and wrath, who inflicted punishment upon those who dared to disobey those injunctions that the hierarchy of the Church had placed upon the common people as representing the demands and will of God.

When the Emperor Constantine adopted Christianity as the state religion of Rome in 312 A.D. it was not because he was a believer in the Christian doctrines, but  it was purely for political reasons. His desire was to destroy the power of his antagonists who were believers in and worshippers of the pagan gods. Constantine made Christianity the state religion to obtain the power and allegiance of the majority of the people of the empire.

The Christians were very numerous and were people of such intense conviction that not even the threat of death could remove or change their beliefs. Constantine knew that once he had gained their allegiance, he would have a following that could not be overthrown by those who were worshippers of the old gods.

During his time in office as Emperor, Constantine never accepted the teachings of the Christians as a revelation of truth or of God. He did not establish the canonicity of the Bible or determine and legalize the doctrines that were declared and made binding by the conventions of the leaders of the Church.

Constantine did, however, give his sanction and official approval, but the doctrines were not established by him because he never became a Christian, nor understood its teachings. This is not withstanding all the fantastical and miraculous things that have been written about his supposed conversion to Christianity.

THE SECOND COMING

Prince of Peace

Iknow that it is expected that I will return as the Prince of Peace to establish a kingdom on earth and take unto me those whose names  are written in the book and destroy those whose names are not therein written (Daniel 12:1). This, however, is not the case because when I brought to light that my Heavenly Father had bestowed upon man the possibility to obtain divine love, never thereafter arose the necessity for the existence or the coming of another Messiah or for me to make a return.

Some Christians believe that at the time of my coming they will be of the elect and become princes and sub-rulers of my kingdom. No, this will never be, for I have already come and am working to turn men's hearts to God and to teach them the way by which they may reach oneness with him.

I never taught my disciples or hearers that my reign would be an earthly one or that I was to be king of the Jews in any other than a spiritual sense. Men will not need me as a visible king with the powers and armies of the spirit world in visible form to subdue the evil that exists. There is no Satan to fight against me or my followers, and the fact is that I am already fighting for the redemption of men's souls. The only devils who are trying to influence mortals to evil thoughts and deeds are the evil spirits of men who once lived on earth and who still retain their sins, and the wickedness and evil that exists in their hearts.

The concept that I am the Judge of the world and that I will come one day to judge it is an entirely false and illusionary one and was never taught by me. I do not have the power to judge, as the New Testament claims, and the passage "For the Father judgeth no man, but hath committed all judgement to the son" (John 5:22), must be interpreted to mean that God does not judge, nor do I, but that man as a spirit sentences himself through the memories of his misdeeds that the law of compensation acts upon. Though, with effort on the spirit's part he may be purged of these disharmonies through a process of purification, and they will no longer be a part of him.

There will be no battle of Armageddon, except as each man or the soul of each man is now fighting the battle between good and evil. This is the only battle that will ever be fought between the Prince of Peace and so-called "Satan". Each soul must fight its own battle, and in that fight the powers of God, by his instruments, will be used to help overcome the great enemy, sin. So you see, it does much harm to those who believe that I, as the Prince of Peace, will come with mighty power and in one fell swoop destroy evil and all who personify it, and thereby do the work that each man must do through his own efforts.

Religion of the Future

There will be a religion of the future, a comprehensive and final one, and it will be founded upon the teachings that I am now sending to the earth. These truths will fulfill all the Scriptures promises of my Second Coming, and in no other way will I ever come to mortals of the earth. These teachings will add to the old beliefs that all mankind can embrace and follow and will lead those who follow them to happiness. This religion will be inclusive of all the other religions, so far as the truths that they contain are concerned, with the addition of the greatest truth of all affecting mortals—the New Heart—the transformation of the human soul to a divine soul.

I know that many things are believed because they are ancient or bear the authority of the sages of olden days, their forefathers or some great saint or philosopher who lived many centuries ago. Such a basis for accepting something as fact, although worthy of examination and consideration, does not of itself afford any certainty of truth. Real truths, whether from ancient times or of the present, are the same truths, for truth never changes or assumes new forms, no matter what may be the condition of mortals in their intellectual or spiritual development. Truths are being revealed today and are constantly being revealed as time goes on, and they should be accepted with as much credence and satisfaction as truths that were disclosed in ancient times.

The minds of men were given to them to exercise by query, investigation and search. Never was it contemplated in human creation that the time would come when man should accept anything as the ultimate truth and cease making inquiries. Truths are so many, so great and so deep that mankind has acquired only a smattering of them. To rest at this point in the belief that there is nothing more to be learned in the way of truth would violate and subvert the very object of human creation.

The churches declare and try to enforce the declaration that it is not possible to discover the essential principles of spiritual truth to any further extent than is already set forth in their sacred Scriptures. Therefore, they claim that it is contrary to God's will for men to seek additional truth. Instead, they should accept without question the particular dogmas and creeds of the churches. This has been the demand of the churches upon their members and, by and large, they have acquiesced without question or doubt. This is a major reason why mankind has not progressed further, not only in its spiritual nature, but also in what may be called its human or natural love qualities. Men have remained satisfied and content to cling to the idea that what was believed centuries ago is the only truth.

One of the most damnable doctrines taught by the churches is that of the unpardonable sin. This doctrine will have no place in the religion of the future, for it is a thing that should have no existence either in the world of mortals or in the world of spirits. Every soul has the possibility to redeem itself, for, you see, God loves those who believe in him just as he loves those who do not believe in him, the only difference being that the believers may partake of His divine essence—love.

Great Millennium

As it is commonly understood, the great millennium is a time or period of a thousand years when peace will reign on the earth and the devil, as it is said, will be bound and not permitted to roam to cause sin, sickness, destruction of souls and the other problems that now so generally beset mortals (Revelation 20:2).

Sin was never created by God, nor is it a product or emanation of God, but is wholly the result of the wrongful exercise of man's free will and his appetites. Mankind has a double set of emotions, one on the basic animal level and the other for the higher living, development and fulfillment of the spiritual values. Sin occurs when man's material desires are permitted to overcome the desires of his spiritual nature. With this comes all the evils, discords and disharmonies that constitute man's manner of living his earthly life. Until these things that are not a part of his original nature, but are the perversion of that nature, are eliminated from his thoughts, desires and appetites, the great millennium will never be established.

As a preliminary to the ushering in of this time of peace and purity, man must cease to believe that it will appear with my coming in a manifested physical way as a mortal conqueror who might come with legions of followers, the noise of drums, the force of arms and greatness of power to subdue my enemies. This will never be, for no man is my enemy, but all are my brothers. I am not making and never will make war on any human being, but only on the sin and defilement that is within his soul. This war can never be waged by the power and force of legions of angels, for so great is the power of God's gift of man's free will and so respected is its freedom of action that there is no power in heaven or earth that can change a sinful soul into a pure one by force, threats or conquering legions of angels, even though they are led by me, which will not happen.

The soul is the real person, and that soul can be made pure and sinless only when it desires and consents that such a condition may become its own. It should not be difficult to understand how the erroneous belief that I will come in the semblance of a mortal conqueror and establish a great time of peace, is doing much harm and is delaying the actual time of the coming of this great period.

The result of this belief upon men is they think that everything is to be accomplished by my work and nothing by themselves, except to believe in my coming and to wait and be ready to be snatched up into the clouds (1 Thessalonians 4:17). Men also claim that I, by my great power and the fact that they believe that I will come again to earth and establish a kingdom, will, in the twinkling of an eye, make them fit subjects (1 Corinthians 15:52).

No, this will never be the way that it will be established, and the sooner men discard this belief and seek the true way to purity and perfection, the sooner the hope and expectations of this time will be realized.

End of the World

No one, whether in the flesh or in the spirit, has the omniscience of God or the vision to foretell what will happen centuries ahead; this power belongs to God only. Thus all the attempted applications of prophecies contained in the Bible of future happenings are futile and without justification.

I know that it is expected by most Christians that the world will someday come to an end (Mark 13:31). The world, meaning the earth, will not have an end in the  sense of annihilation, but will continue to revolve on its axis, have seed time and harvest, produce and reproduce those things that are necessary to sustain life. It will continue to have its appropriate seasons of heat and cold and move along in its orbit as it now does until some change of which I do not know may come and destroy it.

Men will continue to be born, live a short time and die a physical death; then for each person, the end of the world comes and thereafter habitation will be in the spirit world. Since all mortals have to die a physical death at some time, why should it be necessary for God to include in the plan of salvation the destruction of the physical world? For planets and worlds and stars to crash together and be destroyed would mean that the orderly workings of God's laws must be interfered with in order that men might be saved or destroyed.

This will never be, although, there shall come a time of wars and rumors of war and times of trouble such as has never been, and then shall come the end (Matthew 24:6). Not the wars of cannon roars or the bursting of shells or the mutilating of flesh or the making of widows and orphans or the ruthless changing of mortals to spirits. But the wars of the spirits of good and evil, of love and hate, of purity and sin, of joy and despair and of knowledge of truth and belief in error—all to be fought within the souls of men with such intensity and earnestness to create mind and spirit trouble as has never been before.

Then shall come the end of the world, the world of sin and evil, of despair and hatred and belief in error. This is the world that shall pass away, and then the world of truth and love and peace and goodwill shall be established on the earth forever. It will become so peaceful and filled with such love and kindness that it will seem as if the city of God has been lowered from heaven to the earth.

Kingdom of Heaven

As I said when on earth, "Narrow is the gate and narrow is the way which leads to life, and few there be who enter therein" (Matthew 7:14). Now this saying applies to the spiritual world as well as to the material world. So let me urge upon all to seek the straight and the narrow way, for only by it can men come to the full enjoyment of what has been provided for them. I cannot tell you the wonders that God has prepared because there are no words that will properly convey my meaning. However, it was truly said, "No eye has seen nor mind conceived the wonderful things that await the true child of God" (1 Corinthians 2:9).

The kingdom of heaven is a place as well as a condition. There is nothing nebulous or impalpable about it, nor is it a reflection or image of the soul's condition, but everything in it is real, substantial and lasting, and not subject to decay or deterioration of any kind. The many mansions of which I spoke exist in my Father's house (John 14:2) and are real and permanent and not dependent upon the condition of the soul for their existence, although the condition of the soul determines just where it shall occupy and find its harmony and happiness. A provision has been made for the soul to have a place that corresponds to its condition and where it will live and from where it may progress. When the soul finds its habitation, it is a place that has already been prepared for it (John 14:3) in accord with its true condition.

Heaven as a place is real and independent of the state of the soul; otherwise, it would be a place of confusion and of appearances and disappearances without stability or abiding qualities. The mansions are there, and whether or not they shall have occupants depends on the harmony of men with God's laws.

These mansions are made of the most beautiful materials, a substance that you might think of as white alabaster, and are furnished with everything that is suited to make their inhabitants content. Above all is the wonderful quality of love that is always present that fills their souls to overflowing and keeps them in one continuous state of peace, joy and happiness.

Now regarding the words, "It is easier for a camel to pass through the eye of a needle than for a rich man to  enter the kingdom of heaven" (Matthew 19:24). I did not use the word "camel" at all, for it has no association with a needle, and it never occurred to me to use that word, as found in many versions of the New Testament. What I did say was, "It is easier for a rope to pass through the eye of a needle than for a rich man to enter the kingdom of heaven." This would suggest that the rich man who is attached to his earthly treasures would be less interested in things spiritual. Thus, it is conceivable that the poor man could enter the kingdom more readily than the rich man.

This parable evoked the question from Peter, "Who then can be saved?" (Matthew 19:25). I answered that through individual effort and earnest prayer to God, all souls can be saved as well as purified whereby all sin and the desire to sin are eradicated from that soul and, in this way, that soul may enter the kingdom of heaven. This sermon was eliminated by later copyist and revisionists and in its stead they wrote; "with men this is impossible, but with God all things are possible" (Matthew 19:26).

So attractive is the accumulation of wealth and the gaining of fame or position that, when once successful, a man naturally devotes his whole waking time and thoughts to these efforts. As a consequence, very little of his short time on earth is given to thoughts of the higher kind or the cultivation of his spiritual nature. The sin of this is that of omission, and it is a sure one in its results, because the thoughts and efforts used to accomplish material results do not help the development of the spiritual side of man's nature.

When man comes to lay down his burdens and pass to the land of spirits, he will find that he is poor indeed, for the eternal part of his being has little development and his soul is fit only for the place where those who have laid up their riches on earth can go. So you see, entry into the kingdom is an individual matter and depends not upon a man's worldly possessions or lack of them, but upon the condition of his soul. So I say, what good is it for a man to gain the world if he is to lose his soul (Matthew 16:26)?

The kingdom is not a finished one, for it is still in the process of formation and is open to the entry of all spirits who seek it in the way provided. No one will be excluded who, with all the longings of his soul aspires to pass through its gates. There will, however, come a time when the kingdom will be a finished one and then it will close for a time and will be the only place of my love and labor.

When I said, "Work while it is day, for the night cometh when no man can work" (John 9:4), what I meant was while the kingdom is open, the work must continue to complete it with the souls of humans changed into divine angels. When its gates close, the work of the angelic laborers will cease on the earth, they will no longer be needed, for the earth shall be restored to the paradise that it once was.

THE TEACHINGS

First Man and Woman

God created the world and, when I say the world, I mean both the physical and the spiritual worlds. These creations were merely changes in form or composition of what had already existed and will exist forever as elements of the universe. The earth on which you live did not always have an existence as a planet and neither did the firmament, the great galaxy of planets and stars, but they were not created from nothing, nor was there chaos. In God's economy of being there is never chaos; if there were, it would be caused by the absence or failure of God's own laws of harmony, and that does not happen.

The first man and woman were not made of the dust  of the ground, but of the elements that existed in the universe of a different order than the mere dust of the ground (Genesis 2:7). They were made at the same time and not one out of the rib of the other (Genesis 2:22). Therefore, the man and the woman are equal in their dignity and in the relationship they bear to God, and one is of just as much importance in the sight of God as is the other.

The man was created physically stronger and was given a stronger mentality for the exercise of the reasoning powers. The woman, who has less in these particulars, was given more of the spiritual and emotional nature and, an intuition by which she could understand the existence of things just as accurately and even more quickly than could the man by the exercise of his reasoning powers. Each was just as the other in respect to the gifts bestowed and together they were the perfect pair—male and female created with diverse functions and duties to perform in accordance with the perfect workings of the laws of God.

Power and love were theirs and neither was made the superior of the other, nor was the one to be subject to the other and, had it not been for their fall, there never would have been the subjection of the female by the male. With their disobedience and subsequent fall, the animal qualities asserted themselves. The male felt his superiority by reason of the fact that he possessed a greater amount of these animal qualities, and therefore asserted this superiority, and the female, observing that this physical superiority did exist, submitted herself to the male and has continued to do so ever after. As men degenerated, this domination intensified, and for many thousands of years the inequality between the male and female continued, and man remained the master. This degradation continued until man found the lowest place of his degeneracy. When the turning point came, the qualities of the woman became more recognized, but very slowly.

The Jews recognized the equality of the woman in all matters that pertain to the home and domestic life. However, men continued the distinction that had previously existed in respect to public affairs and the qualities of the mind. Women were not permitted to develop their mental faculties and were taught that all matters pertaining to the state or the religion of the race belonged to the male. As a result of this course of life the woman developed the spiritual qualities that were hers to a larger extent, and her refinement and emotional nature and love principle exceeded those of the man to a great degree, and she became in her soul nearer to the image of

God.

As the time approaches when man will return to his former state of purity and harmony with the laws of God, the spiritual qualities will assert themselves and the animal qualities will become subordinated. Then the women will be recognized, not only by the individual man, but by the man-made laws as his equal in every particular, and the further fact will be that she will be his superior in matters pertaining to the spiritual. Then the woman will stand before God and man as the latter's equal and, in the soul qualities, his superior; for in the beginning, in this particular, she was his superior.

Human Soul

Life on earth is an important part of the great eternity of living and should not be thought of as a mere stopping place where the spirit is enfolded in the flesh only for its pleasures and gratification. Life on earth is just a fleeting shadow of the spirit life, but it is an important period of man's existence. The way a life is lived on earth will determine its position in the spirit world and where it will find its occupancy.

The physical part of humans is the result of the meeting of those forces that are contained in the two sexes and, according to the laws of nature, are suited to produce the one physical body fit to be the home of the soul that is destined for it. The body that results from this meeting is intended only as a temporary vehicle for the growth of the soul and does not in any way limit or influence its continuous existence.

The body, of itself, has neither consciousness nor sensation and in its beginning has only the borrowed life of its parents and can exist only so long as the soul inhabits it. The physical body was never created to live forever, and men were never created to live on the earth forever, for a greater and larger world has been provided for their eternal habitation, where things are real and only the spiritual exists. When the body's functions have ceased, it is disintegrated back into the elements from which it was formed.

The earth is a mere image of the realities of the spirit world and exists only as a nursery for the individualizing of the soul. The human soul is a creation of God and not an emanation or projection from God. It was created in the image and likeness of its Creator (Genesis 1:27), although not of the Creator's substance or essence, but of the matter that already existed as part of the spiritual universe.

The creation of the human soul took place long before the appearance of mortals in the flesh. Prior to that appearance the soul had its existence in the spirit world as a substantial conscious entity without visible form or individuality, yet with a distinct personality, so that each soul was different from all others. It also had a consciousness of its existence and of its relationship to its Creator.

When the time comes for the soul to become an indweller in the mortal frame, it divides into two separate component parts, a male and female half of the one soul. The two halves incarnate into their respective male and female bodies and not necessarily at the same time. This separation of the soul is necessary for the individualization of each part of the single soul, yet the two parts never lose that interrelationship or their binding qualities that existed before the separation.

Often soulmates find each other, but due to differences in religion, education, finances and social mores, soulmates may be found but not necessarily acquired, until the condition of the higher is achieved by the lower.

Mere intellectual acquirement is not sufficient to attract and bring soulmates together; only love in perfect harmony can bring about this union. If it is not accomplished on earth, it will be in the spirit world; then they will live and progress together through the spheres of love and light.

I know that it is believed that because of man's greatness that he has in him a portion of God's divine essence. This, however, is not the case, for those qualities that appear to be of the divine resemblance were merely created for the purpose of making man the highest and most perfect of all God's creations. Granted, there are certain qualities that man possesses such as love, wisdom and the reasoning faculties that may be said to resemble the God-like attributes, and so they do, but they are not a part of God, but are merely created in the image and likeness of His qualities.

When physical death comes there is a breaking of the silver cord and with that, all connection between the soul and the physical body is severed for all eternity. The soul is then freed, and protected by its spirit body, which of itself is a creation just as the physical body is a creation. The spirit body exists for the purpose of preserving man's individuality and to shelter his soul both while a mortal and after he becomes a spirit. When the soul is liberated from the physical body, its existence will be forevermore in its spirit body. In the spirit world the soul does not have the power to determine its own destiny or location, it is the laws of attraction and compensation that operate to make this determination.

The new spirit may be met by loved ones with kindness and consolation. This is necessary, for if it were not, the new spirit could experience fear and bewilderment and the unspeakable sensation of being deserted. But eventually the parting must come and every spirit must find its home according to its own condition. Then comes a time when every soul must stand alone in its weakness or strength and realize that no other soul can bear its sorrows or take from it its burdens or enter into its sufferings. No interposition of spirit friends or the love of parents or husband or children can prevent this destiny. Although for a time until the soul has awakened to its condition of severance from the mortal life, these relatives and friends may retain it near the place of its entrance into the spirit world. This place may be one of more beautiful surroundings and happiness than the one to which that spirit is destined. However, this does not last long, for the law operates and as the spirit comes into full consciousness, it hears the call and it must obey.

There is no angry wrathful God sitting in judgement, waiting to pronounce sentence on the soul who has left his earth life behind. The soul's destiny is never final because the condition of the soul is never fixed; as its condition changes, its destiny changes, and thus, there is an ever-continuing opportunity for the spirit to progress.

The incarnation of the human soul into the flesh is the first step in its destined progress from an invisible formless existence to a perfected spirit. A soul on this journey never retraces its steps, its movement is always forward. Although stagnation can occur for a time, still the soul always continues as an individualized spirit in pursuit of perfection and the great goal of oneness with God.

Who and What is God

God is both Yahweh and Jehovah of the Hebrew Scriptures and, at the same time, is the Heavenly Father of the New Testament. This is despite the fact that Yahweh is a God of wrath and vengeance in the Old Testament, and the Heavenly Father is a God of love, tenderness and mercy in the New. Yet they are both the same unseen God, Creator of man who has always been one and changeless.

God revealed himself first to Abraham in the Near East, but this was not the first time, for men of the Far East really were the first to have a conception of God. However, the successful development of the concept of Jehovah came among the Hebrews through an understanding of the laws of conduct toward men given them by Abraham. This was brought to a higher level through Moses, who led the people out of slavery in Egypt. Their liberation was brought about as a result of their great suffering and their inheritance of God as a religious concept. At this time the Hebrews were in a state in which they could be used as a whole people as witnesses of the existence of the unseen God.

The exodus showed the power of God in bringing out of slavery an entire people, numbering many thousands, through the inspiration and courage given to Moses. Many of the legends concerning Moses, it is true, are only stories. However, the fact remains that he did lead the people of Israel from Egypt after forcing the reluctant consent of Pharaoh. Then he guided them hundreds of miles for many years to Mt. Sinai and there in the name of the Most High, Moses received the law of the Ten Commandments for the people. Moses could not have accomplished this great exodus of his nation without the power of the living God, Jehovah.

Many of the Hebrews believed in gods other than the one that Moses declared, as is evidenced in their histories, both sacred and secular. Whenever their God, that is, the God of Moses, did not treat them as they thought he should, they would create idols and worship other gods, even a golden calf. To this day I admire Moses's closeness to God and his faith and courage in steadfastly obeying his commands. As a boy in Nazareth I participated with my parents and brothers and sisters in the observance of the Passover, which commemorates this important event.

The Old Testament writings reveal God as the divinity that rules the universe and, in the narrower sense, the physical world of the earth and of man, and is the arbiter between man and his fellow beings. The prophets of Israel contributed to the elevation of the spiritual concepts of the nation and gave the people and their leaders a deeper insight into the true nature of the Lord. This is to be found in the prophet Nathan, who appeared fearlessly before David, the king, to accuse him of murder and adultery in his relations with Bathsheba. It was Elijah who braved the haughty Jezebel and showed the power provided especially for him by angels to show the power of the unseen, eternal God in contest with the priests of Baal. It was Amos who came to the priests at Gilead to warn the Israelites to repent of their sins, mainly the sins of the rich and powerful who abused the poor and brought them misery and servitude.

Through these prophets the people were able to understand that God wanted righteousness and mercy in their dealings with others, not only amongst their own people, but for all people, including the stranger within their gates, for they, too, had been strangers at others' gates. The people had been taught to trust in the one God and to know him through His attributes and laws, which were the guides the Jews were to follow in their relations with other people and in conducting their affairs. They were given to understand that God was Ruler not only of the Jews but of all people, and that he was to be obeyed.

God the Almighty, is omnipotent, omniscient and omnificent and, as such, has no limitations as a sexual concept, namely father-soul or mother-soul, nor can any human expression be applied in truth to God. When I refer to God as my Father, I do this to indicate the fact that I am at-one with him in nature through my possession of divine love, and I make no reference to any qualities that represent human maleness or masculinity, for these should not be applied to God.

There is nothing in all of nature that men are acquainted with or have knowledge of that can be used to make a comparison to God. For men to conceive that God has a form in any manner resembling that of man is erroneous, and those in their beliefs and teachings who deny the anthropomorphic God are right in their thinking. The true form of God has never been conceived of by men in all the ages, including those who believe in the Bible of the Hebrews as well as that of the Christians.

God is of a form that gives him an entity and seat of habitation in contradistinction to that God who, in the teachings of some men, is said to be everywhere and in everything—in the rocks and trees, in thunder and lightning, in man and beasts, and in all created things and in that which man is said to live and move and have his being.

No, this concept of God is not in accord with the truth, and it is vital to the knowledge and redemption of man that such a conception of God not be entertained or believed. To believe that God is without form is to believe that He is a mere force or principle or nebulous power or, as some say, the resultant of laws, which have been established by God for controlling the universe of His creation. These laws are expressed to men by these very powers and principles to the extent that men can perceive them. Thus, God is behind the force, principle and law that are expressions of His being, and without him they could not exist, and they are dependent and subject to the will of God.

I am enabled by my soul's perceptions to see God and His form, but here I use the words "see" and "form" as the only words that I can use to give mortals a comparative conception of what I am endeavoring to describe. Mortals can scarcely conceive of the form of the spirit body of man that is composed or formed of the material of the universe, though it is usually not accepted to be of such material. It is hardly possible for me to convey to mortals a faint idea of the form of God, which is composed of what is purely spiritual—that is, not of physical material, even if it were sublimated to the highest degree.

God is a soul, not the soul that is in the created human, but the soul that is Deity, self-existent and whose entity is the one great fact in the universe of being. It is a mistake for men to believe that because God has created this or that object or thing, that it is necessarily a part of himself. God's creations are no more a part of himself than are the creations of men a part of themselves. Thus, you will see that in all of God's creations there is nothing of the divine except for the human soul that has sought for and has partaken of God's essence—divine love.

God has a locality from where he works out his purpose of creation and makes the evidence of his existence known to man by the energies that control the universe in which man exists. God is of a form that can be seen only by the soul perceptions of a man who has arrived at a high degree of spiritual development and has taken on

God's spiritual nature. To others, God is unseen and unknown except as his laws and the effect of their operation disclose his being. It must be realized that just because men cannot understand or perceive the truth of God's soul, it does not mean it is not a truth. A truth that is not perceived by mortals, spirits or angels is still a truth, and its existence does not depend upon its being known by them.

In addition, God has a personality, and this is expressed and made known to men by certain attributes that to their consciousness exist in the universe. God is not with men in this personality, yet he is with them in his attributes of power, wisdom, knowledge, goodness and mercy. Life emanates from God, yet life is not God, only one of his attributes that he has conferred upon the objects of his creation. In this way man may live and grow and fulfill the purpose of his design.

Now to some philosophers and scientists and scholars these attributes are their impersonal God himself and, to them, the only God. They mistakenly make the created the Creator, not realizing that behind the expression must be a cause, and greater than the expression must be that from which it emanates or, as some believe, evolves.

I who know, desire to say that these manifested attributes, forces, powers, principles, laws and expressions are not and do not altogether constitute that from which they flow or in which they have their source. God is himself alone. His attributes or expressions manifested to mortals and spirits are the results or effects of the workings of his spirit. This spirit is the active energy of his soul. Hence, the form of God is not distributed throughout the whole of the universe where his attributes may be because God's spirit is manifested everywhere.

As was said by Moses of old, and as was said by me when on earth, God is in his heaven, and it may be surprising and startling for mortals to hear, that God has his habitation and is a self-existing soul-form with a locality, and men do not live and move and have their being in God, but in his emanations and expressions and spirit they do.

Prayer and Faith

God is love, and those that worship him in the spirit of love will not be forsaken. I am my Father's son and am

not to be worshiped as God, nor made an object of worship, and to put God in the background is all wrong. So I say, you must love the Lord thy God with all your heart and soul and mind and your neighbor as yourself (Mark 12:30-31), and send your prayers to God in the name of truth. If any name must be used in supplication, then use only the name of the Father, for his name is high over all and the only name under heaven or earth that can bring salvation to man.

What I have said applies to many other declarations contained in the Bible, such as, "He that believeth on the Lord Jesus Christ shall be saved" (Acts 15:11), and "There is no other name under heaven whereby men can be saved" (Acts 4:12). These are the enunciations of a false doctrine that has mislead a great many of the people who have accepted these declarations as literally true. But, if they are interpreted to mean that he who believes in the truths that I teach, then there is no objection. Even then, the declarations do not go far enough, for people may believe in these truths and that belief may be a mere mental one, acquiesced by the mind's faculties and without the exercise of the soul's senses. If to this mental belief be added the soul's faith, then this doctrine will truly be stated and man will understand what is necessary for his redemption.

Belief and faith are not the same. Belief is of the mind, faith is of the soul. Belief can and does change as phenomena and apparent facts change. Faith, when truly possessed, never changes, for faith possessed by a soul causes the longings and aspirations of that soul to become things of real existence, as the house that is built upon solid rock can never be shaken or destroyed (Matthew 7:24). Believe in God and trust in me, and you will not be disappointed. Pray for divine love to enter your soul so that you will know that you are an accepted child of God.

Of all the important things on earth for those who are seeking peace and happiness and the development of their soul, prayer is the most important. Whenever the opportunity presents itself, one should pray. By this, I mean one need not wait for a special time when not engaged in daily affairs, but pray when you can seize moments when your mind is free, even if only for a second. A long prayer or even one formulated into words is not necessary; with the longing, words need not be used. The longing is quicker than the thought, and sending your longings heavenward will bring result.

God is always open and ready to respond to such longings; even a second of true soul-felt prayer with the longings active is more effective than hours of prayer when such longings are not present. Prayers of the lip or of habit rise no higher than the escaping breath and do not cause the divine love to flow. Remember and realize how futile are all the prayers when the soul's longings and sincere desires are not present. Only soul can call to soul, and the holy spirit will respond when such a soul calls. No mediator is needed or the prayers or ceremonies of priests or preachers. God hears prayers direct and responds by sending his comforter.

Prayers to God call for a response that brings divine love, and with it comes faith and the awareness that a new love is growing in one's soul. Many people understand such faith to be mere belief, but it is greater than belief and exists in its true sense only in the soul. Belief may arise from a conviction of the mind, but faith never can. When one prays for faith, it is actually a prayer for an increase of divine love. Faith is based on the possession of this love and will give the aspirations and longings of the soul real living existence. Faith is not the belief produced from the mere operation of the mind, but comes from the opening of the perceptions of the soul.

God answers the prayers of those who seek help to overcome their unfavorable material conditions. This help is manifested through his ministering angels and spirits. These messengers are always watching and waiting and, when the opportunity arises, they use their influence in the best possible way to bring about the desired end.

If the prayers of men can be responded to, they are. But, should a man come to God seeking power and assistance in, say, the murder of a fellow human, no matter how great an enemy that man might be, God will not give the power or assistance or approve of such a desire. God does not by a mere act of the moment or of a physical character, place prosperity or riches into the hands of men. These things must be wrought and brought about by man himself. Yet, by the workings of God's spirits and angels, mortals are aided in wonderful ways. They can cause other mortals to act in compliance with their influence. This influence is always used for the purpose of bringing about a response to prayers that in their nature are proper and worthy to be answered.

The material or earth-plane conditions are not subject to spiritual laws, but to material laws; yet, in a time of need, the person with faith who prays will be kept in contact with those spirits who have forces that will give strength and courage at the time of adversity. Spirits can also be helpful to mortals because they have the advantage of knowing what will happen in the near future and can tell mortals what may be expected or, rather, what will occur.

Prayers can also remove worry. God will respond to sincere prayers and by the operation of his spirit the aspirant will be relieved of the effect of the cause of the worry on his feelings and mental condition.

God gave men free will to act and, by that very gift, took away from himself any absolute power to force men to do as he wishes. God does not force men to act contrary to their own desires, even though they may be for unmitigated evil. God never makes a mistake in the perfection of his created things even though in the case of man it may appear that way. In giving man the great gift of the power of free will, and in its wrongful exercise, man has caused sin and evil to appear in the world of his consciousness.

There are universal laws created by God that he will not nullify even to protect life. Although he can bring into operation higher laws, that, if obeyed, will neutralize the effect of the lower laws. Thus I say, pray not only for material things that are bestowed by God's angels and spirits, but also for spiritual things that are bestowed by the holy spirit.

Forgiveness

I would like to enlighten you on a subject that is little understood since men first commenced to distort my teachings on the forgiveness and pardon of the Father.

Forgiveness is the operation that relieves men of the penalties for the sins they have committed and allows them to turn from evil thoughts and deeds and to seek God's love and the happiness that is waiting for them. The law of compensation, "That what a man sows that shall he also reap" (Galatians 6:7), is not set aside but, when a man becomes penitent and in all earnestness prays for forgiveness, another and higher law is called into operation. The old law of compensation is nullified as though it were swallowed up by the power of the greater law of love (Romans 13:10).

God sees every act of man and, as I said when on earth, not even a sparrow falls without my Father's knowing it, and the hairs of your head are all numbered (Matthew 10:29-30). Just because men cannot see God, it does not mean that God does not see them, for he does, and their every thought is known to him and taken into account. Surprising as it may be, that account is kept in the memories and consciences of men themselves, and when the time comes for them to render an accounting of their thoughts and acts, no other place or receptacle is sought for or examined to find that account than these very memories.

The memory is man's storehouse of good and evil, and the memory does not die with the death of the physical body. On the contrary, it becomes more active and alive and nothing is left behind or forgotten when man casts off the encumbrance and the benumbing and deceiving influences of the mortal flesh.

The suffering for sins committed is not the result of God's special condemnation, but in each particular case

is the result of the workings and scourging of man's conscience and recollections. As long as the conscience
works, the suffering will continue and, the greater the
sins committed, the greater will be the suffering. This
implies that a soul filled to a greater or lesser extent with
these memories, that for a time, these memories will constitute his very existence. He will live with these memories and the suffering and torment that result from them
cannot leave him until these memories, or the result of
them, cease to be a part of him and his constant compan-
ion. This is the inexorable law of compensation.

In the spirit world when a man has committed sins
on earth, the law of compensation demands that he pay
the penalty to the last farthing. There is no redemption
until the individual makes the effort by struggling and
succeeding to get rid of these recollections, and such rid-
dance can be obtained only by the opening of the soul
and the feeling of remorse and regret for the evils done.
God will respond, for it is true that God helps those who
help themselves. When God forgives, sin disappears and
then only love exists and in its fullness it is the fulfillment
of the law. When divine love enters the soul, it increases
as the leaven in the dough and continues in its work until
the entire soul is filled with it, and then everything of sin
or error is wholly eradicated.

God knows no preference and has no chosen people
in the sense that any particular nation is to be saved in
preference to all others. God does not forgive by the sudden blotting out of sin, and so you should know that neither can the popes, priests or preachers by their mere
pronouncing of forgiveness. This constitutes a deception
and an injury to the penitent who asks and prays for forgiveness. Those claiming to possess the power to forgive
men will have to answer for this when they go to the
spirit world. Then they will realize the truth and the
great deception they have practiced upon those who

were their followers and believers in their doctrines.

Teaching the understanding of God's forgiveness was one of the objects of my mission, and before I came and taught this truth, the forgiveness of sin was not understood even by the Hebrew teachers. They were still believers in their doctrine of old, "An eye for an eye and a tooth for a tooth" (Exodus 21:24). The divine love, as I have described, was not known or sought, but only the care and protection and material benefits that God might have for the Hebrew people.

Two Loves

In the universe of being there are two loves. The human or natural love is the love of the physical universe, and the divine love is the love of the spiritual universe.

The love of man, or natural love, is not one that is sufficient to give the highest degree of happiness that may be obtained either in the mortal life or in the spirit life. This love is of a nature that changes as the ideas and desires of men change. This love has no stability that will serve to keep man constant in his affections. The natural love is a love that may last for a long time, and sometimes it seems that it can never diminish or die; yet, in its very nature, it has not that constancy that insures it will last longer than a moment in time. The mother's love is the strongest of all the natural loves given to humans, and one that appears as if it will never grow old or end. Yet, a time may come when that love will die or cease to retain all its beauty and vitality.

The natural love need not be acquired because every human has it endowed in his soul at the time of its creation. This love is not in its original pristine condition as it first appeared in the souls of the first man and woman.

Since their fall it has become tainted and needs to be purified and expressed through kind thoughts and deeds, patience, caring, forgiveness, mercy, and generosity. The natural love is the driving force behind all human love—motherly love, brotherly love and its highest expression, soulmate love. These loves are provisions that are necessary to enable man to work out his progress through the mortal life and in a way that will produce the greatest harmony and happiness among mortals as they contend with the difficulties, cares and disappointments of their earthly existence.

Now, the divine love is a very different love from the human love. Divine love is not the development of the human love, but is the essence of what love is. It was never conferred upon man as a perfected or completed gift at the time of his creation, but is a love that is waiting for him to acquire through effort and aspiration. This love is not a part of man's nature, but could be obtained and possessed ever since the time of my coming by all who seek it. God has always been the same, with the exception of conferring his divine love on man at the time of my birth when he revealed himself truly by revealing his greatest attribute—love, which is his nature.

Divine love comes from without and is not developed from within. It is the result of individual acquisition and not the object of universal possession. It may be possessed by all or it may be possessed by only a few; each man must determine that for himself. It is not a matter of right, nor is it ever forced upon one. It is greater than hope. It is the substance of faith.

There is no royal road to obtain divine love; all must pursue it in the same way as I taught when on earth. The opening of the soul to God through sincere longing and prayer and the divine love will flow from God's soul to the human soul carried by the holy spirit. Once it is implanted, it finds lodgement therein for all eternity. It may lie dormant for a time, but can be awakened when the soul desires.

When man possesses divine love, he possesses everything that will make him not only the perfect man, but a divine angel. Then he will understand the moral precepts of brotherly love and also of the oneness of God. He will not have to seek further those qualities that bring peace and goodwill, but will know that every soul is his brother. Envy, hatred, strife, jealousy and all other evil qualities will disappear and only peace, joy and happiness will remain. Man will then be able to "Do unto each other as he would have the other do unto him" (Luke 6:31), without effort or sacrifice on his part, for love worketh its own fulfillment and all its beneficence.

Divine Love is the greatest thing in all of the universe and not only the greatest, but the sum of all things, for from it flows every other thing that brings peace and happiness.

I am a progressing spirit, and as I grew in love, knowledge and wisdom while on earth, I am still growing in these qualities in the spirit world. When the love, goodness and mercy of the Father come to me, they come with all the assurance that never in all eternity will I cease to progress towards the very fountainhead of God's love, the only God, the All-in-All.

Your brother and friend,

Jesus

Divine Love

Oh perfect love, that you could be mine
and quell this yearning for all time
pray hold not back but flow to me
So one day I may divinely be

Please hear me Father when I cry
from my humble home to your kingdom high
no other has love like yours to give
Oh love come to me and forever live

Lift me above earth's mortal pull
let life no more my senses dull
fill me with love and take my hand
let me learn and understand how

Your Divine Love will draw me closer
to you as no other love has power to do.
So hear my call Father hear my plea
and let your love draw me closer to Thee.

Olga Johnson
Lincolnshire

THE TWO LOVES

HUMAN LOVE	DIVINE LOVE
ENDOWED ⟷	BESTOWED
IMAGE & LIKENESS ⟷	SUBSTANCE & ESSENCE
PURIFICATION ⟷	TRANSFORMATION
BELIEF OF MIND ⟷	FAITH OF THE SOUL
KNOWLEDGE ⟷	WISDOM
HAPPINESS ⟷	JOYOUS FULFILLMENT
LIMITED PROGRESS ⟷	UNLIMITED PROGRESS
ENLIGHTENMENT ⟷	THE CHRIST PRINCIPLE
ETERNAL LIFE ⟷	IMMORTAL LIFE

This chart compares the qualities and the benefits that are acquired from the two different spiritual paths of love revealed by Jesus. Eternal life means that in all likelihood the soul will exist forever. Immortal life means that the soul that has acquired the substance of God and become one with God is assured to exist as long as God exists.

PSYCHIC INFLUENCES IN THE BIBLE

Compiled by Austin D. Wallace (1951)

Apports

Numbers 11:31 17:8
Psalms 78:24
Ezekiel 2:9

Casting Out Spirits

I Samuel 16:23
Matthew 8:16
Mark 5:8
Acts 5:16 8:7 16:18 19:12

Clairaudience

Ezekiel 13:13

Clairvoyance

Genesis 15:1
Exodus 24:10
II Kings 6:12
Jeremiah 1:11,13
Ezekiel 8:3
Daniel 2:19 3:25
John 21:6
Acts 9:10,12 16:9

Dreams

Genesis 28:12 31:11, 24
37:5, 9
Samuel 28:15
Job 33:15
Matthew 1:20 2:13 27:19

Fire Manifestations

Genesis 19:24
Exodus 3:2 14:24
Judges 15:14
Daniel 3:22
Acts 2:3 7:30

Gift of Healing

Matthew 10:8
Luke 9:2 10:9
I Corinthians 12:9 12:28

Healings

I Kings 17:22
II Kings 4:35 5:14
Matthew 8:13 12:13
Luke 5:17 9:11 17:14
John 5:8-9
Acts 3:7-8 9:18 14:10
28:8-9

Holy Spirit

Joel 2:28
Acts 2:4,17 4:31 9:17

Independent Spirit Voice

Genesis 21:17 22:11,15
Exodus 19:3 20:1
Judges 2:1 13:3
I Samuel 3:4 9:15
I Kings 19:5
Job 4:12
Ezekiel :24, 25, 28 13:13
Matthew 17.5
John 12: 28-30
Acts 7:31 9:7 11:7-9

Independent Writing

Exodus 24:12 31:18 34:1
Deuteronomy 9:10
II Chronicles 21:12
Daniel 5:5

Inspirational Speaking

Mark 13:12

Levitation

Kings 18:12

Ministering of Angels

Genesis 21:7 32:1,24
Joshua 5:13-14
Kings 19:5-7
Luke 1:26 2:9,13 4:10
Acts 5:19 8:26 12:7

Names of Controls

Genesis 32:29
Judges 13:17
Job 26:4
Mark 5:9

Physical Phenomena

Genesis 30:30
Exodus 4:3
Judges 6:40
Kings 19:5-7,11,12
II Kings 3:15
Matthew 8:26
Acts 12:7

Prophesy

Exodus 4:17
Samuel 10:6
Ezekiel 14:13
Luke 1:67-68

Seances

John 20:19
Acts 2:1-4

Spirit Guidance

Exodus 4:15-16
Acts 11:12
Galatians 2:2

Spirit Light

Genesis 15:17
Exodus 34:29
Ezekiel 1:28
Acts 9:3

Spirit Manifestation

Genesis 3:8 18:1 19:1
I Samuel 28:13-14
II Kings 3:15
Ezekiel 2:2
Luke 1:11
John 21:4,14

Spirit Materialization

I Kings 19:6
Luke 25:15-16
Acts 26:16

Spirit Power

Daniel 6:22
Matthew 28:2
Acts 5:19

Spiritual Gifts

Daniel 2:26
John 14:26
Act.s 2:17
Luke 10:19-20
I Corinthians 12:1,4

Tongues

I Corinthians 14:18

Trance

Genesis 15:12
Numbers 24:4
Daniel 8:18 10:9
Acts 10:10 22:17

Trumpet Mediumship

Revelations 1:10 4:1

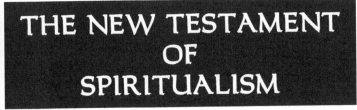

THE NEW TESTAMENT
OF
SPIRITUALISM

I hope you have found *The Genuine Jesus* of interest and of value. Its purpose is to serve as an introduction to the vast legacy of spirit communications by the two American mediums, James E. Padgett and Dr. Daniel G. Samuels. If you  would like to continue reading, the follow-up book is *The New Testament of Spiritualism*.

This voluminous work contains eye-opening accounts from Jesus, his disciples, the Gospel writers, and a great array of people from throughout history. Some note-worthies are Moses, Elijah, St. Paul, Socrates, Nero, Elizabeth I, Francis Bacon, Martin Luther, John Wesley, Napoleon Bonaparte, Emanuel Swedenborg, Abraham Lincoln, Stainton Moses, Ralph Waldo Emerson, Mary Baker Eddy, Queen Victoria and many more. Discover scientific, philosophical, historical and spiritual concepts you have not read before. Learn more about the origin of man, the human soul, soulmates, the spirit world, spirit progress, the nature of God and much more. Gain insight and knowledge from this book of extraordinary depth and spirituality.

To order the 515 page *The New Testament of Spiritualism* please post a check or money order payable to Ross Publications:

Within the UK £12.95 inclusive to:

Mrs D. Pilgrim
79, Binyon Crescent
Stanmore
Middlesex
HA7 3NE
lovepilgrim@aol.com

Within the US $24.95, Canada $28.95 USD inclusive to:
Ross Publications
734 1/2 New York Street
West Palm Beach, FL 33401
alanross@aol.com
561 833-0384

Lightning Source UK Ltd.
Milton Keynes UK
UKOW06f1809030616

275567UK00021B/332/P